Extra Dry, with a Twist

Extra Dry, with a Twist

◆

An Insider's Guide to Bartending

Shaun P. Daugherty

Twenty-year veteran in the restaurant/bar industry

> DARREN —
> ENJOY THE INTERACTION WITH THE GROUP!
> ENJOY THE BOOK!
> Shaun P. Daugherty

iUniverse, Inc.
New York Lincoln Shanghai

Extra Dry, with a Twist
An Insider's Guide to Bartending

Copyright © 2008 by Shaun P. Daugherty

All rights reserved. No part of this book may be used or reproduced by any means, graphic, electronic, or mechanical, including photocopying, recording, taping or by any information storage retrieval system without the written permission of the publisher except in the case of brief quotations embodied in critical articles and reviews.

iUniverse books may be ordered through booksellers or by contacting:

iUniverse
2021 Pine Lake Road, Suite 100
Lincoln, NE 68512
www.iuniverse.com
1-800-Authors (1-800-288-4677)

Because of the dynamic nature of the Internet, any Web addresses or links contained in this book may have changed since publication and may no longer be valid.

The views expressed in this work are solely those of the author and do not necessarily reflect the views of the publisher, and the publisher hereby disclaims any responsibility for them.

ISBN: 978-0-595-46697-9 (pbk)
ISBN: 978-0-595-71284-7 (cloth)
ISBN: 978-0-595-90993-3 (ebk)

Printed in the United States of America

Contents

THE MAN BEHIND THE BAR.................................vii
ACKNOWLEDGEMENTS......................................ix
BEFORE WE BEGIN...xi
WHAT IS A BARTENDER?...................................xv

Part I THE TWO PHASES OF BARTENDING

PHASE 1 THE BASIC PRICIPLES OF BARTENDING..........3
1. Proper measures for drinks.............................5
2. Serving the customer..................................9
3. Keep your co—workers happy.........................11
4. Knowing and memorizing your common drinks......15
5. Be a host to all that enter your establishment.......18

PHASE II THE BARTENDER PSYCHE......................19

Part II TEN RULES THAT MAKE A GREAT BARTENDER

1. BE A PROFESSIONAL.................................25
2. YOU ARE IN CHARGE................................29
3. EVERYONE IS YOUR BUDDY........................33
4. BE A GOOD LISTENER...............................38
5. POUR A GOOD DRINK...............................41
6. KNOW YOUR CUSTOMERS' DRINKS................44
7. PROMOTE, PROMOTE, PROMOTE..................46
8. KNOW YOUR COMPETITION.......................50

9. BE AN ENTERTAINER 53
10. BE ETHICAL AND RESPONSIBLE 55

Part III   FIVE THINGS TO STEER AWAY FROM AS A BARTENDER

1. DRINKING WHILE YOU WORK 60
2. RELATIONS WITH YOUR COWORKERS 66
3. PERSONAL BUSINESS AT WORK 70
4. STEALING FROM THE OWNER 73
5. COMPLAINING IN FRONT OF YOUR CUSTOMERS 77

Part IV   THE PERSONALITIES

1. I AM HOLIER THAN THOU 87
2. THE SOCIALITE 90
3. THE JEKYLL AND HYDE SYNDROME 92
4. THE CASANOVA 95
5. THE STORYTELLER 98
6. THE CON ARTIST 100

SOME FINAL THOUGHTS 102

THE MAN BEHIND THE BAR

He deserves a hero's medal for the many lives he's saved
And on the roll of honor his name should be engraved.
He deserves a lot of credit for the way he stands the strain
And the bunk he has to swallow would drive us most insane.
He must pay the highest license he must pay the highest rent
He must settle with the agents, though he doesn't take a cent.
And when it comes to paying his bills he's Johnny on the spot
He'll pay for what he sells you whether you pay him or not.

And when you walk into his place he'll greet you with a smile
Be the worker dressed in overalls or the bankers dressed in style.
Be you Irish, Dutch or French, it doesn't matter what
He'll treat you like a gentleman until you prove to him you're not.
He must listen to your arguments that happen in his place
And show no partiality for any creed or race.
The bunch outside can knock the King, the Kaiser, the Czar
But he has to be neutral—The Man Behind the Bar.

It matters not the aches and pains and hardships he endures
He doesn't tell you his troubles though you always tell him yours.
And if the weather is hot or cold or turns from rain to snow
It's up to you to tell him so, he ain't supposed to know.
Should he sit down to read the news, some fool with half a jag
Pulls up a chair beside and begins to chew the rag.
"Tough job", they say, "have patience" a more patient man by far
Than Joe could ever hope to be—The Man Behind the Bar.

Yet the preachers in the pulpit and the lecturers in the hall
Will tell you that the churches are against him one and all.
But when the church decides to hold a neighborhood bazaar
They start selling tickets to the man behind the bar.
Yet the time will come when he must shuffle off to mortal soil

Hang up his coat and apron no more on earth to toil.
When Saint Peter sees him coming he will leave the gate ajar
For he knows he's had his hell on Earth—The Man Behind the Bar.

—Anonymous

ACKNOWLEDGEMENTS

Without the help from some family and friends, I would not have had the drive to finish this project. I would like to thank the following people that gave me the encouragement needed to complete this book. A special thanks goes to Hayley Kirk, who undoubtedly gave this book the foundation needed to give it that book feel. She helped with the editing throughout and I could not have done this without her. I would also like to thank all of the people that read the book as it was going through its metamorphosis. Thank you for taking the time out in doing so. Without that and the critiquing throughout the process, it wouldn't have gotten to the final product it is today. Of course, let's not forget all of the people that inspired me to write this book: many people that I have had the privilege to serve and entertain, and to those I have enjoyed working with and for throughout the years. They were the inspiration. There would have been no knowledge and stories to complete this book if they did not turn the tables and entertained me on occasion. I also learned what I know from the different types of people that I have had the opportunity to call my clientele. I appreciate the many years of fulfillment that you have given me. And of course, let's remember those that were not so pleasant: the scoundrels, thieves, and all around bad people. Though, at the time it did not seem to be a good thing, you had your hand in making me a more rounded individual.

I would not have lasted as long as I have in this business if it weren't for all of the great bar owners I had the privilege of working for all these years. I have been fortunate to work for many whom, in their own right, were very good bartenders. They understood the pros and cons of the business and were there to have your back when something would arise. They were also great teachers; people that I would go to if I was unsure about something. I will be forever grateful for your willingness to teach.

Some other people I would like to thank: Cliff DeCamp, who has been my friend and sound board for many years—thanks for always believing in me. My wife, Brenda, and children, Ciara and Kiera, who have tolerated my hours in front of the computer writing this book, and the many bartender brothers and sisters out there who have been down in the trenches with me and understand my reasons for this book. Of course let's not forget the parents. I am fortunate enough to have two sets: my Mom and Tony and Dad and Marylou. Thanks to my younger siblings for keeping your older brother in line throughout the years.

A toast: To all those who have enriched my soul and have given me the knowledge to be who I am today. Salut!!

BEFORE WE BEGIN....

Let's start by saying that I believe that there are many reasons why a book like this needed to be written. A high percentage of our society feels that to be considered a bartender; one should only possess some knowledge of mixing drinks and have a minimal background with wines and beers. Though these are some of the fundamentals of bartending, and do need to be mastered when you are working behind a bar, this is only a small portion of what it takes to be successful in what can be a very rewarding occupation. Admittedly, it will take time to get a full grasp as to what are the essential skills needed to reach your full potential. It can take many years of trial and error, and seeing what fundamentals best fit you, to achieve what you want in this profession. It will also be up to you to realize when you erred, and what you have to do to make yourself better at this job when you do.

What you are about to read was written to help you shorten the time getting from the "person who serves drinks" to what should be considered a "bartender". Just like any occupation that has a good upside, it will take time to reach a level in which you will be looked at as a master of the trade. This public view will give you every opportunity to be successful by giving you the positions in this field that most bartenders would give their left arm for. Bars of many types will be calling you for your services due to your professionalism and demeanor. Though many not in the know dismiss this job as a profession—that is exactly what it is. Bartending has become less idealized as a respectable occupation. It is up to someone in the know to set the record straight. It is up to someone to give this profession back its glory. Hopefully, by the end of this book, people will see what is truly involved in doing this job correctly and they will begin to look at it a little differently.

As the title denotes, this book contains insights to give you the foundation to become one of the best in your field. Other than giving you several hundred recipes to memorize, since I feel that this has been overkill the last couple of decades, the following pages in this volume will give you a glimpse to the other side of the job: the human side. These insights are opinions and are not based on studies other than the ones that I have done to improve my own skills as a bartender. The insights that I am about to share have provided me every opportunity to make more money than if I had memorized my book of drinks. Like the books you see that "Give you better Abs" or "Give you a better nest egg for retirement", this book contains my opinions and observations. However, if you follow these thoughts, you will be further ahead. I believe that I have compiled a book that will give you a strong foundation—a foundation that you can build a good career on.

Some of the points that I will share can take you many years to realize. My first five years in this career were a blur. If I had only taken the job a little more seriously in those years, I would have been much further ahead today. These pitfalls can destroy you quickly if you let them. I was one of the fortunate. Not only am I ALIVE today—I am hoping that I can shed a little light on what you can do to stay away from the things that could have ruined me for life.

First thing to remember when entering this occupation is that you are human. Usually, your objective when entering the bartending industry is to do this only on a temporary basis. You, by no means, see yourself doing this for the rest of your life. Some of the reasons for bartending are to fill the void between jobs, pay for school while you are getting the education needed in the field of your choice, or you are doing it to meet more people in your life. These are all good reasons to get into the bartending field. However, I must stress that this job, in itself, is a real occupation. If you go into it looking at it as a true occupation, and give yourself the opportunity to learn all aspects of the business, you can make a lot of money. If you decide that this profession is not for you on a permanent basis, you will at least know that you have the skills needed to perform the tasks at hand. You can use these skills if you ever need to get back into it in a pinch. Once you know the overall concept, it will be like riding a bike. It will only take you one night to know what the people of the establishment are drinking. Without the following views, it could take you many more to get the other part of the job down. That is why it's important to have a solid foundation. You will always have that foundation if you were to come back into the business. You can start where you left off. From there, you can add on to what you previously learned.

Another human element that I mentioned a little earlier—one of the foremost reasons young people get into this business—is the party factor. Those who enter this occupation and do not realize that bartending is a job will fail and probably lose more than just their job when doing so. As you will read in the coming pages, there are many opportunities that can steer you on the wrong path when bartending. You must always make sure to have this in the back of your mind at all times. That way you will be ready to question yourself whenever these opportunities present themselves. Some of the guidelines I describe will help you keep going in the right direction. Awareness is half the battle in everything.

I have been in the bar/restaurant business for over half my life. When I am not working behind the bar, I like to, on occasion, go and check out other bars and see what's happening. I love to meet new people; one of the things that's kept me in this profession for so long. However, I am at a loss when I see the lack of quality and inexperience behind the bar nowadays. It makes you wonder what the owners and managers are thinking. When did this profession lose its style and grace? When did they decide to only pay a waitress/waiter salary to the people on the other side? Since when did the occupation of bartender not seem to be a trade to the people making the decisions in these establishments?! Do I seem outraged? I hope so! If not, I am not making my point.

Many bar owners and bar managers feel they need to have sexy and young individuals behind the bar. To have this, and to pay them server pay, they have to hire inexperienced people. Sure ... sex will sell for a little while. But, eventually you will attract nothing but people looking for the opportunity to get lucky with this individual. You will not attract, what I feel, is a loyal clientele—people who not only come in for the bartender, but also for the camaraderie of the fellow patrons that the skilled person behind the bar has attracted. Little do owners and managers realize how many more good customers their establishment would have if they would stop looking at the hourly wage and began looking at the big picture. Hey, I'm all for a good looking individual behind the bar. Just make sure that being good looking isn't the only thing bringing the people into the establishment. Experience, as you will know when you complete this book, is not only beneficial for the bartender. Being experienced will enhance the amount of money a business will bring in in the long run. Pay your bartenders what they are worth. Not only will they be grateful; they will show their loyalty to the establishment by bringing in the right clientele. Loyalty goes both ways in this business. Pay yourself forward by bringing in the right person that will attract the right patrons.

Though I will miss some points in the coming chapters, I hope you realize the most important moral that I am trying to get across. It is imperative to be a well rounded human being in this line of work. A well developed character will give you the best jobs in the industry. This book will help you understand the psychological side of this business and gives you the tools to build from so you, in time, can become one of the considered elite in this field of work.

I hope you enjoy and learn as much reading this as I've enjoyed and learned writing it. I share some secrets that will help you be successful. With this new found success you will be rewarded with higher tips and a better clientele. All it takes is a little dedication on your part to make this happen.

Cheers!

WHAT IS A BARTENDER?

This is something that seems to be misunderstood by the general public in this day and age. Anyone who serves drinks from the other side of the bar is generally looked at as a bartender, and has been given this title out of default. One who is in the know will tell you otherwise and for good reason. Serving drinks is only one of the many things that are part of this interesting job. There is so much more to be realized when you are working behind the bar.

Bartending is one of the oldest and most underrated occupations in the history of mankind. Many who have had the privilege to be on the other side have had the opportunity to serve and befriend the many masses who have stepped foot in their establishment. They have become the confidant, the friend, to the many of those who would otherwise have nothing else to do with their free time. They have been there to listen to the many stories people would share with them, all the while knowing that if the person requests their story not be shared with the public, it will not be. A bartender is also a servant to his fellow man—knowing he is no better or worse than the man or woman he's serving. However, he is there to satisfy your every request and feel a sense of fulfillment when doing so.

Be it the businessman in his finely finished clothing, to the man who just worked at the construction site, the bartender has become the person they first want to see and converse with after a long day at work. Want to hear the newest joke or the latest breaking news? Go in to see your favorite person at the local pub and have some good conversation while winding down with a couple of beers—or maybe something with a little more kick.

How is a bartender able to bring different types of people, living different types of lifestyles, under one roof? How does a bartender manage to have everyone having fun with one another, when they would probably not have any association with each other in any other type of environment? A "bartender" will have learned through trial and error that most people come to their establishments to be more than just another face at the bar. In fact, most patrons are there for the camaraderie of their fellow man. They are there to meet new people and have some type of social status within these four walls. It is up to the bartender to give his followers the comfort in knowing that they belong.

A bartender is usually the anchor of any institution serving liquor. For the most part, he or she will have the say on whether the establishment will be a popular spot or one that barely survives. The type of clientele that frequent the bar will be the choice of the person who does more than just serve drinks behind the bar; it will be someone who really cares about the people that he has had the privilege to call his clientele—his customer base. And yes—the type of clientele in their establishment IS the choice of the bartender if he/she knows how to act with the people that could eventually become other regulars at his place of business. The person occupying space behind the bar will be the entertainer, the conductor, the listener—the many facets that will make this complicated, yet simple man/woman a "bartender".

When a bartender goes on the other side to be the provider of the spirits, they have been thrust on a stage. Not only are they there to be the one who quenches the thirsts of the patrons that sit at the barstools—they are there to put on a show. This could very simply be a good and heated conversation with a couple of the local politicians. Or it could be him trying the timing out on a joke he just heard with a couple of the regulars that come in to see him on a frequent basis. It could also be him giving someone advise on what to do while they are stuck in town for the next couple of days due to a boring convention or visiting with the in—laws. If you like the art of "flair bartending", you will find some that will show you some tricks with the bottles; just so they know everyone has been served to their contentment before doing so.

A bartender is a jack of all trades and a master of none. He is able to change his personality depending on the type of person he is dealing with at the time—all the while, keeping a nice and refreshing smile on his face. He is educated, though not to much, on all of the topics of conversation; educated enough so he doesn't have to taste his size twelve shoe most of the time when talking different subjects with his customers.

There is much more to it than most people think when entering this occupation. To be a bartender you will need to master the art of people. You need to master this above all else to be given the title and stand proud knowing that you have accomplished much more than learning how to make drinks. Once you begin working on the other side, you will realize that there will be many mountains to climb, many hurdles to overcome to be considered a success. When you have that figured out and actually begin to dive into the things that will make you one of the elite in your profession, you will come to understand that it will be up to you to be a success. It will be up to you to be the person that people will come far and wide to see.

So … what is a bartender? One day, with the right frame of mind and the commitment to be one of the best, you will be able to look in the mirror and the answer will be right in front of you.

PART I
THE TWO PHASES OF BARTENDING

PHASE 1
THE BASIC PRICIPLES OF BARTENDING

The occupation of bartending, like all other occupations requiring skill and knowledge of a trade, takes some time to get good at. At one time, not too long ago, bartending was looked at as a skilled trade. Even if the experienced bartenders thought you had the right character to be in this business, you still had to work your way up the ladder, and be good at the other facets of the bar and restaurant business, to get the opportunity to experience the job first hand. For instance, some establishments would start you waiting tables for a time. This would give the management the opportunity to see how you faired dealing with the general public one table at a time. Waiting on tables requires you to be good at time management. You must be able to multitask. It could be costly to not know when the food is ready at one table, and when it will be time to take an entrée order at another. You must manage to keep everything in sync. You should look at each table as a project—with an understanding that you could have several projects going on at one time. If you don't, you will keep everyone you are serving on edge. This will equate to bad tips and questioning yourself whether or not you are capable of working in this business in the first place. Serving tables also helps train you in the proper etiquette of serving wine, cognac, or any other drink. All of the above will be beneficial to you when you do get the opportunity to work on the other side.

Once the management felt you were above par at waiting tables, they would go to the bartenders and ask if they felt you were ready for the next level. If everyone agreed, you would then become the bartender's aide—commonly known as the bar back. A bar back is someone who does all of the grunt work for the bartender. You are there to empty trash, wash glasses, put away glasses, keep the bar stocked, etc. You will usually see people doing this in the very busy establishments. You must have someone doing this job to keep everything going at a nice steady flow. While doing the grunt work, a senior bartender would take you under their wing and begin teaching you the basic principles to be accepted for this line of work; accepted by the other bartenders and, most importantly, the crowd that you will eventually be serving in your establishment. Even at this point, becoming a bartender wasn't something that was just handed to you. You had to show you had the right mind set to be considered for this illustrious occupation.

Let's go back and define the term "basic principles". You must have the basic principles down to do an adequate job behind the bar. Adequate is only average as far as I'm concerned. If you are looking for average reading this book you are wasting your time. But, having these down will start you on the road to be given the title of bartender. Until you have earned the right to be given this title, you will still have many hurdles to overcome to be considered one of the best. Bartending is a lot like the martial arts. It takes constant fine tuning to hone in on what it takes to be the best. It will take more than what I, or anyone else, can teach you. You have to have the inner workings to be a great bartender. Some are born with it and some have to work hard to get there. This is something we will go more in depth with in later chapters.

In the next several pages, we will go over some of the basic principles of bartending. Without these skills, and getting good at them, you will not be able to move to the next level.

1. Proper measures for drinks

To keep everything in line with the inventory, and to keep the boss happy, it is imperative not to forget this when first stepping behind the bar. You must keep the measures, for the drinks you will be making, by what is instructed in the book of recipes. You will come to know the inventory of your bar very well. It is important to keep the inventory in sync with sales at all times. Not doing so can easily put the bar into a tailspin and have you out of a job due to the bar closing. Our first and most important responsibility is to make sure that this does not happen.

You would not know this from the above paragraph, but, I am not an advocate of computerized pours, measures, and weighted spouts that are supposed to pour a perfect shot every time. In my experience with these gadgets, I have found that they are more unpredictable than human error. I also feel that you are taking away some of the talents of the bartender when using such devices. A real skill in this profession is being able to pour a true shot whenever asked, and doing this "free—pouring" it out of the bottle using your basic pour spout.

There are only a few places where the controlled ways of pouring work. Most of these places are those where the bar is not the first priority in terms of making money for an establishment. The bar is only there to serve the purpose of keeping people around longer to spend more money. A few examples of these are: gambling casinos, cabarets, and movie houses. You could probably get away with it at a night club that serves a younger crowd. However, the crowd will eventually find a place that serves better drinks when they find out that the drinks being served here are being automatically measured, and not poured with the skill of the seasoned professional behind the bar. Once the word gets out, you will have to close the bar due to not having customers.

Even though the bartender is not pouring more booze than the recipe calls for, they are giving that illusion when free—pouring. When people see that you aren't using any types of measuring devices, they feel that they are getting more than they paid for. When you use the others, people feel like they are being shorted. Though that is probably not true, that is the subconscious feeling that they get. It will also wear badly on your tips. "Why should I give you more of a tip if you're not giving me more?" could be their philosophy.

Another positive reason for free—pouring liquor is that you can add or subtract liquor, (in moderation of course), to give the customer the flavor that they are wanting in their drink. This is almost impossible to do with the measured pours. Just remember to always keep your inventory in mind. This is one thing you, as a bartender, should never lose sight of.

When you are first getting into bartending, it is imperative to learn how to free—pour. There is a very easy way to make this as second nature to you as breathing. These following steps will get you where you need to be:

a. Take an empty liquor bottle, (preferably liter size), and fill it at least half way with water. This will give you the feel you want when pouring from the bottle. Put the same type of pour spout you should have on all of the bottles at your bar: your basic pour spout with no measurement gadgets that will hinder your pour.

b. Proceed to grab a one ounce jigger and pour a shot of water into it from your practice bottle. You want to grab the bottle at the bottom of the neck, (the top, thinner part of the bottle), and tip it to where the bottle is tipped at about a 45 degree angle so you get the right flow. You want to believe that there is liquor and not water in the bottle. This way you will concentrate on the amount of time it takes to fill this one ounce jigger. When you are doing this, come up with a count to see how long it takes. Everyone will have their own count, (we will go more in depth with this at the end of this lesson). Dump the water you have just put into the jigger into the sink. Repeat this ten times so you can get used to your count.

c. After you feel comfortable with your count, move onto a rocks glass. Take your practice bottle and free—pour a shot into the rocks glass using the same counting method you should have become accustomed to while pouring into the jigger in the previous step. When you are done pouring the shot, take the rocks glass with the shot of water and pour the contents into the jigger and see how you did. Repeat this ten times.

d. Repeat this lesson everyday for the first month. It's always good to do this right before your shift begins so you have it down. Once you get more comfortable with your count, and it is becoming second nature, keep your skills fresh by doing this once a week. This will keep you finely tuned and it will give you the consistency you need to do your job properly. After doing this for 20 years, I still keep my skills fresh. Don't ever lose focus. It will save you from under or over pouring when it's most important.

Until you get this skill down, you might want to use a jigger. This way you won't be second guessed when the inventory is off. You will have covered yourself and will save the bar from losing money during your learning process. Also, shots should be whatever the bar regulates as a shot. It could be one ounce, one and one-quarter ounces, or maybe one and one-half. Be sure to follow the guidelines that the bar has established when pouring a drink.

Let's go back to what a "count" is. A count is yours and no one else's. I have heard, on numerous occasions, a bartender describing to another about a drink having "a three count of vodka" or some other type of booze for that matter. How does that bartender know how fast or slow the other is counting to make his measurement correct on that particular drink? A count is what you come up with in terms of how long it takes you to free—pour a shot. You might feel comfortable saying—"one Mississippi ... two Mississippi ... three", or just counting up to a certain number to reach your goal. The way you do it is completely up to you and what you feel comfortable doing. But, it is very important to stay consistent. Stay with the same count you started with at the beginning. That way you will eventually get to the point where you will not need to count. You will get so good at it that you will pour a shot automatically. Your subconscious will take over the task at hand due to repetition.

There is another term that is used quite frequently behind a bar that is used when you want to know how much of a certain ingredient will go into a particular drink. This term is called a "part". A part can be any measurement. A part is self descriptive—it is part of the whole in a drink. For example: you know that there are three parts to a drink and the recipe calls for two parts of vodka, that tells you that the drink consists of two-thirds vodka and one third something else. There can be seven, ten, or even only one part to a drink. It matters on what drink you are making, and how many ingredients are in a drink, to determine how many parts make a whole. This term will be used frequently when working behind the bar. It is important to remember this meaning. A good example of when the word "part" comes into play is when you will be making a larger volume of something. There are many establishments that have specialty drinks. They will make an abundant amount of that particular drink in advance to save time.

I once worked in a place that pushed margaritas for *happy hour*. To save us from having to make these one at a time, we would make a couple of five gallon buckets. Knowing that a margarita is made with two parts tequila, one part triple sec, and two parts sour, we knew that had to put only half the amount of triple sec versus the other two ingredients. This will give you the same drink as you would have had if you were to have that drink made for you as a single serving. This is where the term "part" is the most effective behind the bar. You will see this term used for recipes for food as well, so the person making the food can make the quantities needed, depending on the amount of people eating, without ruining the recipe.

It is your responsibility, as a bartender, to understand what a true shot is. A typical shot is one ounce of liquor. However, I have worked at places who felt that a one and one-quarter ounce was a shot of liquor. No matter what, a drink should never consist of more than two ounces of liquor. There are two main reasons that this is or should be the rule: One—controlling the inventory at the bar and ensure you are not undercharging for the amount of liquor your customer is getting. Two—you are responsible for the effects your drinks have on your customers. You do not want a patron to get a DUI or possibly get into an accident on the way home. With the laws now enacted in several states, you and your establishment could be found responsible for the actions of that individual. The two ounce rule also includes drinks such as: Long Island Ice Teas and Martinis. One ounce of 80 proof liquor is considered one serving in the eye of the law.

Free—Pouring—The art of pouring the proper amount of liquor from the bottle using only a basic pour spout and without the aid of a measured or computerized pour.

Jigger—A small measuring cup for liquor, usually made out of stainless steel or glass, that usually consists of measurements of one and one half ounces and one ounce; made for the purpose of putting proper measurements of liquor into a drink.

DUI—Driving Under the Influence of alcohol or drugs. You are considered under the influence in the continental United States if your blood alcohol level is at or in excess of .08 percent.

Happy Hour—Pertaining to the allotted time a bar has discounts on food and drink. Happy hour, which is usually more than an hour, is usually in effect between the hours of four pm through nine pm to attract people just getting off work.

2. Serving the customer

As a bartender, the customer always comes first. Keep in mind what your job description is. Your occupation is to serve the people that come through your front doors. That is it. Everything else that you do behind the bar is just setting you up to serve the customer to the best of your ability. Why are there glasses to clean and fruit to cut? Why do you have to restock? The reasons are that you need to do these things to keep the customer satisfied. Customers who are satisfied will come back and bring people along with them next time; just so their friends can meet their friendly neighborhood bartender. If you take care of them, they will become your regulars that only come to see you and no one else at this establishment. The patron of the bar is very powerful. The existence of your bar hinges on the satisfaction you are able to give to him or her when they come in to visit this place of business. So, you better take care of them.

This next rule is true in all aspects in life. This rule is a bit microscoped in the food and drink industry. The rule: You can do all things right most of the time—but, it only takes one error to put a bad taste in someone's mouth that will last a lifetime. It is human nature to look at the bad things in the forefront of the good things. People are looking for any excuse not to like something. That is why that it is very important not to take your customers for granted. If you do, the crowd will go where they will get the service they expect. It will be very hard for you to win them back when this has happened.

To assist you in making sure that you keep everyone happy, here are some points to keep in mind to get the respect from the clientele you are serving:

- Never have someone wait more than thirty seconds for a greeting from you. Even if you are busy at the time, and they have to wait a little longer for a drink, at least they will know that they have been seen and that you will be with them shortly.

- Always make sure that you never make a customer wait any longer than two minutes to have a drink, unless it takes longer for you to make the drink properly. If it takes you longer due to being too busy, you might want to think about having two bartenders working instead of one.

- When a customer has finished a drink and has put the glass on the rail, (the part of the bar closest to the bartender which is typically lower than the bar itself), that usually means that the customer is ready for another one. However, always ask the first time you are serving a particular customer. Though most old timers will give you a hard time for not knowing the rule, it is important not to waste and to be a little naïve. Most of the new generation of socialites are unaware of this rule and are only setting the empty glass in this location to get it out of the way. Better to play it safe by asking.

- Though a bartender depends on tips for a majority of his wage, do not assume that the money on the bar is a tip. Some people lay money down to pay as they go. They will tip you when they get up to leave by leaving it under their empty glass. If someone new sits at the recently vacated spot, before you get a chance to clear the space, have the manners to ask politely if the money happens to be left by the last patron. Never, ever, assume.

An easy way to ensure good service is to always put yourself in the shoes of the customer. How do you want to be taken care of when you go into an establishment? Always treat the clientele the same way you expect to be treated when you get the opportunity to go out and be a patron yourself.

Note: If you happen to have a bar that serves a large amount of frozen drinks, and you are blending these as they are ordered, it would be viable to have an extra bartender to make those types of drinks. This will ensure the rest of the customers will have good service and will keep them from waiting a long period of time for their own drinks. Another time to have an extra bartender is for a restaurant bar that has a busy bar and a good drinking crowd eating at the tables in the restaurant section of the establishment. This extra bartender can be used as the server's bartender. They would be in charge of making the drinks for the servers, so the other bartender can concentrate on the bar crowd. This will not only keep the patrons at the bar happy—it will keep your co-workers and their patrons happy.

Be sure to have enough stations set up to accommodate each bartender. A station should have each of the following: a tub of ice with an ice scoop, a well liquor rack, garnish tray, juice and soft drinks. If there are two bartenders and only one station, you will only be slowing down the system. This makes having more than one behind the bar redundant and very costly for the establishment.

3. Keep your co—workers happy

To live in harmony is all most people want to do at the work place, no matter what occupation they happen to be in. You will spend more waking hours with the people you work with then with the family at your residence. So, why not do what you can to make your waking hours as enjoyable as possible by keeping everyone at work happy? You do this by doing your part on shared duties. You should be a team player and do the things you can to ensure a smooth and care-free day. It makes your employment more tolerable and gives you a sense of acceptance with the co-workers. Why fight it? We all must do our part to keep everyone happy.

The same logic applies to a bartender. Though most of the job will consist of dealing with the public who decides to sit at the barstools in front of you, there is much work to do to make sure you are serving the patrons properly. The term "side work" is used to describe the duties that are performed to keep the bar going in fluid motion. There are things that are needed to be done to prepare for the next shift coming in. "Why the next shift?" you ask. If the previous bartender did the side work that they were supposed to do, they will have already completed the things that are needed to be done for the shift you are now working. This way, you would not run out of the things necessary for you to have during your shift. If they did not do these duties, you would run around with your head cut off trying to catch up, while trying to keep the customers satisfied. This can become very stressful. This would also keep you from doing the duties that were assigned to you for the next shift. As you can imagine, this could affect many shifts that succeed the one that failed to do their part.

Once you fail to meet the least amount of requirements that are needed for that next shift to go well, you will have started a war of words between you and the person who will be relieving you. You will no longer be living in harmony with your work family. "One bad apple can ruin the barrel" saying comes to mind. Everyone will be at everyone else's throats because of one lazy individual. One bit of good news: This person will not last long. He/she will be ousted by the other bartenders eventually. This example of laziness tends to happen more than once, usually, and the others will finally understand what's happening and get rid of the weakest link of their team.

Doing the job that is asked of you to the fullest, by doing what is needed for your fellow man and woman, will speak volumes on how well you work with others in this team-oriented occupation. It will be an important view on what is to become of you in this line of work. You must play well with others in this job.

To best understand what is involved with side work, I have listed some of the daily and weekly chores that must be done by every bartender. With the daily chores, all bartenders have their hand in those. Weekly chores are divided and shared so all of these get done. Some jobs are easier than others. It is best to rotate work, so no one gets stuck doing something they don't like. This will cause another stir within the family.

DAILY CHORES

1. Keep the bar stocked with full coolers of beer and wine. Make sure to put the newest stock behind the already existing stock to ensure freshness. There is nothing worse than being served a skunk beer, or a vinegary wine, at a bar. ROTATE! ROTATE! ROTATE! If you happen to have open bottles of wine, always check their integrity before your shift by smelling and tasting them. If the wine is bad you will know almost instantly. Better you taste it before your customer does. Check liquor bottles so you know that the person relieving you will have enough of all the types of liquor for his shift. Just to save the next person time and frustration, always backup a bottle that has less than a quarter of booze remaining in it. The liquor bottles always tend to go empty at the most inopportune times.

2. Empty all trash cans and bottle cap tins at the end of your shift, so the next bartender is coming in fresh. All of these should be sprayed out with detergent and water on a nightly basis and put back in place in the morning after they have dried out. This will keep the bar from smelling like old beer and booze. You will always know which places don't do this when you step foot in their establishments. If smoking is still legal in your establishment, be sure to always keep clean ashtrays on top of the bar. Never empty ashtrays in the trash; always dump them into the cap tins in case you still have one burning.

3. The mats behind the bar should be cleaned with detergent and sprayed with water and placed somewhere to dry overnight. The daytime bartender will put them back in their place. This is another thing that tends to be forgotten and will cause the bar to have that raunchy smell. Mop the floor of the bar at night with soap and water.

4. Cut enough garnishes so that you have enough for you and the shift that will be relieving you. DO NOT OVER CUT. Though it may take time, you will know what amount will be used on a daily basis. It's good to have the fruit as fresh as possible for a couple of reasons. One of these is so it looks good on

the glass's rim of the drink that you will be serving a customer. Secondly, smell is fifty percent taste. You want to have a nice fragrance to go with the drinks that you are serving the customer. Though the majority of fruit cutting goes to the people working the first shift, the night shift must make sure you have enough fruit to hold you over until the end of your lunch rush.

5. Make sure all of the mixes are filled and not outdated. The containers holding the juices should be replaced with clean ones on a daily basis. Always have the dishwashers of the establishment, (if you are so lucky to have any), run these through instead of you trying to clean them in your dishwater. You want to have these go through the heat to kill off any bacteria that may have collected through the day. It is everyone's responsibility to check on the freshness of the juices and the cream before their shift begins. All soda and draught beer should be checked to make sure the next bartender is stocked. Make sure pressure of the CO_2 is where it should be.

6. Have all of the glasses that need cleaned washed and put away before you are relieved from your duties. Start the next shift with new water in the sinks. It is important to change the water in the sinks at least once an hour to keep the water at the temperature that it's supposed to be. If you are cleaning a lot of glasses, try to change the water more frequently.

There is much more that can be added to the list. All places should have two lists for the bartenders to follow. The lists are "Daily Side Work" and "Weekly Side Work". Some of the Weekly Side Work activities could be cleaning out the condensers on the coolers to keep them from overheating or cleaning brass. These lists will ensure a nice and clean establishment and will keep everything running smoothly.

The group of bartenders in each establishment should have a say what and what not should be part of the list. To make sure everyone has a part in the cleanliness of the bar, the group should have monthly meetings to tweak the lists and make them realistic and workable. It will also be important for everyone involved in the daily and weekly duties to have a say as to what chores should be included. This will make sure that everyone involved will do their fair share in the activities.

A little tip: A secret to keeping the water at the temperature required by law without burning your hands, and to keep the glasses you have just washed from steaming up, is to make the third sink that has the sanitizer solution in it cold. This will be the last sink that the glasses will be dipped into. Put the three sanitizer tablets, you will be putting into the third sink, into a small glass of scolding water. Once they have completely dissolved, dump the solution into the cold water. Before grabbing dirty glasses to begin the cleaning process, dip your hands into the cold sanitizer sink. This will give you a cold, temporary shield on your hands that will give you more time to do a more thorough cleaning of the glasses in the most important part of the cleaning process—the first sink with the hot water, soap, and glass brushes. To ensure proper cleanliness, once you spin the glass on the brush and get the glass soapy, run your fingers around the ridge of the glass where lipstick and debris from the garnish seems to always be left behind. This will save you from the embarrassment of serving someone a drink with a glass that is not properly cleaned.

4. Knowing and memorizing your common drinks

When you finally get an opportunity to look at a book on mixed drinks, you will come to the conclusion that there is absolutely no way on this earth that you will be able to memorize every drink. Not only will you see that to have the ingredients for everything in the book, you would need twice the space. There will be drinks in there that have probably been made only a few times and never made again. There are only one out of ten that will be listed in the book which will become a household name. Fewer will become a household name for a longer period than a year. Each and every day there is a new concoction made—at least given a different name. The bartender that came up with a drink will either make it only for that one customer who thinks that it's the greatest thing since sliced bread, or they will forget to write what they put in it to make it taste the way it did the first time. The ones you will see in the books, that you will eventually buy, are from those fine mixologists who had the hindsight to write down the recipe and send it to the proper authorities. If the person in charge of editing the book felt it deserved the ink to be printed in the next publication, it would be added to all of the others who received the same review at one time or other.

My point is this: There are way too many drinks to learn them all and new ones being invented on a daily basis. The best thing that you can do, as a bartender, is to learn the old stand-bys. There are drinks out there that have been made for generations that any bartender should know how to make. You have your Old Fashion, Manhattan, Martini, Margarita, Long Island Iced Tea, etc. Learning the common drinks will save you a lot of time looking for recipes when you are too busy to even think straight. One way to know what these common drinks are, versus the not so common, is to ask an old salt who has been in the business for a while. If they like you, they will give you a list that you can work on and build from as you're getting your feet wet. Another way is to listen to the drinks that are being called for at your establishment while you are working. Which ones seem to be more common than others? This way you will know which ones you should be concentrating on more. This will give you a starting point. Each establishment will have specialties that you should memorize as well. These drinks may be made at other bars, but are known by different names. There is a reason that these are specialties: they are commonly made at these establishments; they have proven themselves as good sellers. Make sure to make this first priority in your memory bank.

There is something else that you will realize when you work on the other side for a while. Drinks that you thought you knew how to make will change. A couple of years ago, as I was working at a bar in Wisconsin, a gentleman at the bar asked me for a "Sex on the Beach". When this first came out when I was working in Texas several years earlier, it was a shooter that consisted of Midori, Chambord, and Pineapple Juice. When I put this drink in front of my customer, you would have thought that I had just started my first day at the bar the way he looked at me. "Buddy, didn't you understand what I was asking for?" he quipped. "You asked for a Sex on The Beach, didn't you?" was my response. Come to find out, the common way for these to come nowadays is on the rocks, and without any of the original ingredients that it had called for when I had originally made it. Always keep up to date with the new way things are being made by subscribing to trade magazines and buy books that will give you yearly updates.

The main reason for writing this book was to stay away from teaching you drinks and going more into the other side of the business, so I will keep this very brief. There are some drinks that are usually called out by their contents at the bar. It is always good to have their given drink names in the back of your mind when someone wants to test you. Below, I have named a few off the top of my head, that I felt would be probably used:

- Cape Cod—Vodka and Cranberry Juice with a Lime
- Greyhound—Vodka and Grapefruit Juice
- Cuba Libra—Rum and Coke with a Lime
- Screwdriver—Vodka and Orange juice
- Sea Breeze—Vodka, Grapefruit Juice and Cranberry Juice with a Lime
- Bay Breeze—Vodka, Pineapple Juice and Cranberry Juice with a Lime
- Madres—Vodka, Orange Juice and Cranberry Juice with a Lime
- Red-Eye—Beer and Tomato Juice
- Mimosa—Champagne and Orange Juice

There will be others, no doubt, that you will come to know once you get some experience under your belt.

Be sure to have some recipe books available behind the bar when you are working. No matter how long you are in this business, you will find your nose in them from time to time; not to only learn what's in that drink for that very instance someone calls for it, but to also come up with a special of the day to give the customers something new and exciting to try. You might find some old bottles of something in the liquor cabinet that you have no use for until you find a recipe for it. You will want to start your own personal Rolodex of drinks that you can take with you from bar to bar. You will always have someone ask you for a drink that they had that is not found in any book. Perhaps it was invented by the guy at the bar next door. Keep a note of it with this directory that you can make for yourself.

If you are unsure what a drink has in it, and you don't have time to look it up, never be embarrassed to ask the customer calling for the drink. If it's something that they enjoy, there is a very good chance that they will know what goes in it. It will save you from taking the extra steps and will get the drink to the customer quicker.

It is important to know what tools you will be using frequently, so you can keep them in a location that is convenient when you are making drinks. Remember: Try to make as few steps as possible when making drinks. It will give you more time in front of the customer. Those few extra steps will slow you down to where you will keep the next customer waiting too long for their drink, which can hinder them wanting to come back to the establishment.

5. Be a host to all that enter your establishment

As a bartender, you will have many things to be responsible for. Not only are you there to serve your patrons their favorite adult beverages. In most cases, you will be the first line of communication between an individual coming into the establishment and someone who works there. You will be the person responsible for giving this new customer their first impression of the place. You could be the first one on one contact that this person has had since entering the front door. As in most situations, the first impression can be the most meaningful one of them all. This could be the moment when this person will realize that they will become a regular of the establishment or a one time visitor. Your demeanor and how you take care of this customer is important for this very reason. Greeting every customer with genuine kindness will enhance your chances of success. This is what a true bartender does: they make the room their own. You are the host to all those that come into your room. Not one person is more or less important than the other. They are ALL important.

There are many types of bars in the world. The reason for this is the same reason there are many types of flavors of ice cream, many types of automobiles, many types of homes to live in. We have selections because we all have different tastes that satisfy us. It would be a very boring world if that were not the case. It's nice to have a selection. But, the same philosophy rings true in all of these establishments. The customer will come back if they feel that they are being treated the way they should be treated. You are a big part of the decision on whether or not a customer will be back in. There was a reason they first stepped into the bar in the first place. Make it your mission to get each and every person that you serve a reason to come in there a second time—and to bring in others when they do.

You are getting close to understanding that we have just begun the long process of becoming a bartender. You are now ready to dig a little deeper. You now have the basic fundamentals to achieve the success that you are working toward. Now it is time to get into the finer points and move on to Phase II.

PHASE II
THE BARTENDER PSYCHE

Once you have the basics down, you are now getting into the nuts and bolts of this occupation. This phase is what will keep everything together; it is the glue that is needed to bond you and the patrons that enter your lair. Bartenders that are to remain in this business, and want to be successful in this trade, will become the experts in this phase of development. This is the time when you should come to the realization that there is more than just knowing the basics to be as successful as you want to be. It will become evident that you have only pealed the surface layer of what you will find to be a several layer occupation.

To be a bartender, you have to have the right personality; you have to have what it takes from within your character, something that cannot be taught by me or anyone else, for that matter. To handle the ins and outs, you must have the state of mind that gives you the edge. You must be able to handle anything that's thrown your way, good or bad. For the remainder of the book, there will be stories from my life experiences that will give you examples of what I'm talking about. The poem at the very beginning of the book gave you a short and witty summary of what a bartender is. This section of the book, as well as the following chapters, will help guide you though this phase of development. This phase will be instrumental on showing you how to follow the principles that will help you become a great bartender.

There are many questions that will arise when you get to this level of growth. There is a very common thing that happens when you reach this point of learning: self-doubt. The questions that you have will eventually give you the understanding that you are ready to move forward and more in depth with knowing the bartender psyche. They will help you take the next initiative to get you where you want to be.

Here are some of the questions you will be asking yourself:

- *How can I bring more people into my bar and keep them coming back in?*

- *What do I need to do to attract the type of clientele I want to have in my establishment?*

- *How can I make more money without working more shifts than I do now?*

- *What can I do to be one of the best in my occupation?*

- *What can I do to be a good example to, not only my customers, but to the people that I work with on a daily basis?*

- *I am doing everything the way it has been taught to me. Why am I not seeing the results I want to see and bringing in more people?*

You have learned what you feel is everything you need to be successful as a bartender. You assume that the basic principles should be enough to get you where you want to be in this line of work. Not only would you be wrong on that assumption, but once you realize how much farther you need to go, and how much more you can do to improve on all that you have been taught, you will come to understand that you have not yet come even close to being a "bartender". Have you ever looked at a bartender, that has years of experience under his belt, and wonder how he built the clientele that he has? Have you ever wondered why you like a certain bartender more than another when you go into an establishment? Believe me when I tell you that at one time, these successful bartenders were in the same place you are now. They came to the realization that they needed to be more than your average neighborhood guy serving drinks to make the real money. They had to work their way to the point that they eventually had everyone coming in to see them. It doesn't happen over night. It takes some time and experience to know what will, and what won't, work for you. All bartenders have there own traits to give them the upper hand on their fellow tenders. Each and every success has its own story. The men and women who have become the elite will tell you that they got there a little differently than the other. But, they all will have the same advice to tell you: You must have the right state of mind to be on the other side; you must be on the top of your game at all times.

As I stated in the last section, this occupation is a lot like being in the martial arts. Congratulations! You have achieved a green belt. Now, you must take the knowledge you have and mold it into what will make you the best you can be. What you will learn as you move along the path of being the best, if you decide to take the right path, will give you the knowledge you will need to become a high degree black belt. Remember this: You have to make the lessons you learn in this book your own and enhance them. Books can only teach you so much. As the title of this book states—this is only a guide. It is up to you to form your own opinions and what will best fit you as you move forward.

If you were to look at the many occupations in this world that deal with the public, you would see that a large majority of the successful people in these jobs were at one time behind the bar and were very successful in this trade as well. They had come to understand the element that is needed to have such success. They had to open their inner selves to understand the human element of this and any other social job. To be above average in any occupation dealing with people, you must have this element to have the success that you want to have. I have always said that part of the requirements to obtain any job, you should have to work in the bar and restaurant business for a solid two years. That way, to pass the class, you would have to learn this skill. It would definitely make this world a much better place if everyone had a more acute understanding of human nature.

What is human nature? Well, it's amazing how the time you spend working behind the bar can give you a better understanding of this. Each and every one of us has our own quirks that make us unique. We each have our walls that we try to hide behind. To be a great bartender takes someone that gets the fact that these quirks are what make every individual interesting. It takes someone who understands when and if the personal walls can be looked over every once in a while. It's an incredible feeling when you have people beginning to come out from behind those walls for you. That's when you know that you are beginning to come of age and becoming someone that may have a shot at doing this—be someone more than just that person serving them a drink.

As you read through the following pages, you will understand the things that it takes to go above and beyond in this line of work. Once you have this down, you will not only see your wages and tips grow, you will see yourself grow as a human being.

For those of you who are not going to make bartending an occupation, I suggest you read the following pages anyway. That way, you will look at the person that is serving your next drink differently. You may also be able to use some of these words of wisdom in what you're doing in your line of work. There's nothing wrong with digging a little deeper into your own psyche to find a way to improve. Once you have a better understanding as to what is needed to be successful, you can use these things in the everyday happenings of your personal life. Having the right frame of mind will work wonders in more than just your job. Being positive and keeping a level head will work wonders in everything you do.

PART II
TEN RULES THAT MAKE A GREAT BARTENDER

1. BE A PROFESSIONAL

The occupation of bartending is a very entertaining and a very social occupation. If you don't keep your guard up, it is easy to get caught up in the party and forget why you are there in the first place. A bartender must always maintain order in the establishment and not engage in any risky behavior with the clientele. Professionalism is a must in an environment where alcohol is served. You are there to be the example to those around you. This includes having the proper etiquette in terms of how you dress, how you speak, and how you perform your duties. To get a full grasp of what all of this means, you must look at this as what it is. You are being paid to be a bartender—the gate keeper to the place of business. You are there to make sure that everything is running smoothly; to make sure nobody goes to the extreme. To do this you must understand that you are a professional. You are getting paid to do a service.

To be a professional at this job takes a lot of self—control. It is easy to lose sight of who you are and why you are here. Before making sure that everyone else stays at a level of social acceptance, you need to make sure that you, yourself, don't go to the extreme and must always keep a level head. If you don't, you may find yourself looking for other work.

One case in point occurred when I was working with one of the most organized people in the profession. During the day, she was in charge of maintaining the stock and ordering whatever ran short. She worked hand and hand with the chefs and the bartenders to get a better overall understanding of what type of stock needed to be on hand at all times. When she was in charge of this I don't recall ever running out of anything. If a discrepancy ever arose with the inventory, she would find it almost instantaneously. Along with her inventory duties, she kept the books and scheduled the front of the house—making sure that she had a plan "B" if anyone were to ever call off sick. She was a meticulous employee that kept a close watch on the inner workings of the establishment. She was a "professional" at her job.

Her biggest downfall occurred after one of the night bartenders decided to walk out on his job one evening. Instead of hiring another bartender, or overworking her existing staff, she decided to pick up a couple of shifts in order to make a little extra money. At the time, that didn't seem to be a bad idea. It would give her a better understanding of the inventory by seeing what was being used, and what wasn't, and would give her an upper hand when it came to reordering. Working a couple of shifts behind the bar is a strategy I myself would recommend to any manager as a way to "kill two birds with one stone".

However, this individual fell prey to what I like to call the "Jekyll and Hyde Syndrome". The bar was considered to be a pretty happening place at night. We started getting college kids that liked to come in and indulge in several shooters. To have a better appreciation of the story, let's just say that the bar didn't only attract the younger drinking crowd. It was perceived as a neighborhood establishment that people would visit, to eat with their families, or to have a few cocktails on their way home from a hectic day at the office. It was a place well liked by all age groups and social circles; a true example of what a neighborhood bar is.

Being one who likes to be social, I went in to see how my friend was doing on her first night being behind the bar. Figuring she didn't have much experience serving the public, since her job during the day consisted mostly being behind the scenes, I figured I could give her a hand if she got too flustered. Plus, it gave me an excuse to hang out with some of my favorite people and actually have a couple of drinks with them on their side for a change.

As I entered this fine establishment, at the heat of happy hour, I witnessed a large group of college guys rooting on someone at the bar. As I got closer, and saw who they were cheering on, you could here the sound of my chin hitting the floor echo throughout the room. It was my co-worker, the perfect example of professionalism during the day, doing body shots with these young studs as she lay across the bar. So I wouldn't make a scene of my own, I decided to grab my own drink and let the rowdiness die down a bit before relieving her of her duties. I didn't want to embarrass her on her first night on duty—though she did a good enough job of that on her own. To quiet the ruckus that had been going on, I figured if I sat next to the action, it would sway the crowd from going any further with the activities. I wanted to take the slow and easy approach, so I wouldn't make a bigger scene.

It wasn't long after I sat on the barstool to take my first sip of foam from my newly poured beer that the owner of the establishment walked in. He couldn't have come at a worse time. If you could have seen the look he gave me, it would have paralyzed the strongest of men. It took me quite a while to gain any respect from this guy again. I looked like I was part of this fiasco! I finally convinced him otherwise.

For the young and intelligent associate who decided to try to earn some extra money—she wasn't as lucky. Not only did he catch her in the act of going over the line and partying with the clientele, she was probably the drunkest and most out of control person in the room. The person that he had entrusted, to take care of the most important duties of the establishment, had not only lost her dignity this night—she had lost her job as his right hand person. She had lost sight of being a professional. She had forgotten that she had a job to do.

The presence of the college students stirred things up and led to some rowdy behavior, not just amongst the students, but the previously described individual as well. She switched behaviors once the students came in and convinced her to start participating in the drinking. Her responsibility as a bartender, and a watchman, vanished when she started to party with her clientele. How are bartenders able to accurately measure and serve drinks when they are more intoxicated than the customers? The answer is that they can't. It's crucial to remain conscious of your duties, so you can keep the company from losing customers and losing money.

As in any profession, you should strive to be the best that you can be. When it comes to bartending, you play host to people that are out to enjoy themselves. You must stay focused on the job at hand. I have seen a few souls lose everything trying to keep up with the clientele on a nightly basis. This business will suck you dry if your objective is to get drunk while you work. Being behind the bar is like have a loaded gun with an unlimited supply of ammunition. If you are not careful, you may find yourself with a hole in your head. Not drinking while you work will be more drawn out as we go deeper into the book. It will become realized early in your career that this is one of those things that you do not do to be the best. Keep this in your inner thoughts at all times: The customers are supposed to be enjoying the spirits—not the person serving them.

Another part of being a professional is your appearance. You must fit the atmosphere that you are working. Meaning—you should present yourself well in front of the type of clientele that you are serving. If your patrons consist of middle aged yuppies that are dressed for success, you should be well groomed and wrinkle free. You should keep yourself looking your best at all times. If you are working at a night club that serves rockers that have the long hair, maybe give yourself a look that will present itself well with the people coming in. You must fit the environment for which you're part of.

No matter what your look or style is, you should always be fresh and clean when working. You are serving the general public. Have respect for yourself, and your fellow bartenders, by not smelling like you just bundled fifty bales of hay. If you are working with another person, you will be closer than comfort on a couple of occasions, nightly. You do not want to have this person question if you had showered that day. You definitely don't want your customers to question it. This will surely stop them from coming in when you're working. It is always a good idea to have an extra shirt handy in case of a big spill, so you don't have to answer the same question, about the cherry juice stain, fifty times.

Professionalism isn't only about physical cleanliness—it's about mental cleanliness as well. You need to understand that you should keep the language behind the bar at a "G rating". You might be having a conversation with someone at the bar that could care less. However, Sister Mary from the convent down the road might be having lunch at a table with some neighborhood folk. You do not want to say anything that will disrupt her enjoyable meal. She and all of the other church going folk who come in to eat could give a rat's you know what that you know a few flavorful words. It's your duty to make everyone's visit enjoyable. So, keep it clean darn it!

You're probably asking yourself a couple of questions regarding a "G rated" bartender. "How is he/she going to be able to tell those great bar jokes?" or "How can a bartender do their job without swearing someone out on occasion?" In conversation, it is vital to keep your slang and dirty vocabulary away from general chit-chat. You want to be looked at as an intelligent individual. Plus, you have no clue to whom you are talking to and who has good ear shot on the talk you are having with the masses at the bar. But, in most cases with all other things in life, there are exceptions to the rule. When you are about to dig deep into your box of jokes, just make sure that everyone within listening distance will not feel uncomfortable when you are telling the jokes. Be sure to ask everyone around the area if it would be okay. If it isn't the right time, the people that want to hear them can wait until the coast is clear. When it comes to giving someone what they deserve in a heated conversation, it is best to do this in private and not around the others at the bar anyway. Heated conversations tend to stress everyone out—not only the people on the wrong end of the talk. The innocent bystanders will only laugh and joke about it to make it okay in their minds. It relieves the anxiety that they feel at that moment. Try to keep your composure in the public spots where others could be caught up in something that makes them feel uneasy.

Being a professional at your work place, no matter where that may be and what you do for a living, is the way to be. It keeps you out of trouble with customers and the co-workers. It can give you job security as well. It shows the people in charge that you not only care about the place you work, you care about presenting yourself well in whatever your occupation is.

2. YOU ARE IN CHARGE

With all of the responsibilities that you will learn you have when working behind the bar, you should put it on yourself to have total control with everything that happens in your place of business. It should be the bartender that makes the calls with the clientele. If you feel someone is stepping out of bounds in your place of business—causing bad blood and disturbing the rest of the clientele—you have to take control of the situation. You need to remove this person from the establishment before he or she causes more damage than what they have already caused. This will give the other patrons the comfort in knowing that you are there to keep this a nice and relaxing refuge from their everyday lives. They will know that they will be able to enjoy the place without worrying about a fight starting up the next barstool down. They will know that you are there on patrol to ensure their safety.

There is much more to being in charge than just this. However, this will be a good starting point. I have witnessed incidents on too many occasions where the bar owner or manager will allow a bad seed back in the bar after the bartender has gotten rid of him and told them to never come back. The owners and managers should read this book thoroughly or find another profession. They need to trust the bartender's judgment as a professional in the matter, and abide by what the bartender concludes on problematic customers. You are not just there to fill a shift, but to regulate any situation that happens while you are there.

I was a frequent regular of a bar down the road from where I lived. Not only did I like this place because it was a nice and easy walk from my home; this place had a great mix of neighborhood folk and there was always stimulating conversation you could enjoy while sipping on a beverage. The bartenders in this place were top notch—true to the title that they had been given. They were very personable and would welcome new customers to their establishment by introducing them to the regulars. In my opinion, it was a perfect place where I could unwind and enjoy the barstool after hours of serving people on them. There's nothing like finding a place where you feel at home. Every time I walked in, I knew that I would find some people that I enjoyed hanging out with. You would even see the priest from the local catholic church every once in a while, enjoying good conversation with the locals—something you could always find in this pleasant establishment.

One night something out of the ordinary at this pub happened. A fight broke out with a couple of guys that normally didn't come in. They had been kicked out of the pub they normally frequented earlier that night, so they happened to find our oasis. The bartenders did the right thing and kicked these rowdy individuals from the establishment right away. But, the next day while the owner was in, these individuals came in and apologized for causing the commotion the night before. There are two sides to every story and the owner had just heard the one side. Without considering his employees' points of view, the owner allowed the offenders another chance. After a few more disputes, the bar had become labeled a place in the neighborhood as a punch palace—a place where fights were always breaking out. Once all of this started happening, the good clientele began to go elsewhere and the bad seeds, who were not allowed in any other establishments in the area, started infiltrating this once prosperous establishment. Within six months of the first occurrence, the bar had lost all of its good business, closed, and went on the market. The cancers of society had overrun and killed the bar.

The bar owner was more concerned about losing two customers and forgot to realize the big picture. He had forgotten what his bartenders were hired to do—run and take care of the establishment as if it was their own. I have had the privilege of working for some great bar owners who understood the philosophy that the bartender is there to keep everything under control and should have a say on who can be a customer and who cannot. Allowing the employees this right influences the customers to always be on their best behavior, not only with the boss, but also with the people working at the bar.

If a customer is getting a little out of control, don't ever question doing the right thing by giving this person an early exit. The fools who tend to get in these bad situations could care less what you feel anyway. Don't ever have second thoughts in your decision. It's amazing how the fights tend to disappear once everyone realizes you are not taking any crap. Don't get cocky and act like you're the second coming when you are doing the right thing; just act how you would if it was your own place of business. This way you are always doing what's best for the establishment and the good clientele who keep it in business.

I must add that it is important to call 911 when things go out of hand. Do not become the hero and think you can take a couple of people on when you have to stop a fight. These mortal enemies become very close allies once they realize what you are attempting to do.

There is much more to being in charge than what we have already discussed. It's important to give you these points, as well, to give you the full perspective. Being in charge and in control relates to liquor inventory, a balanced cash drawer, taking incoming calls, and the list goes on. It's important to have the control needed to handle all of the things that will be thrown at you.

Being in charge of the liquor inventory is the main function for you in the eyes of the owner. It must be understood by the bartender the cost vs. retail in the liquor inventory. Drinks that you serve behind the bar are usually marked up a certain percentage point, typically starting at 300% for your top shelf liquor and your bottled beer. This is the amount needed so the bar owner can break even at the end of the night. That's why it is vital to know where every ounce of drink is going. Being a bartender automatically gives you the responsibility of this. You must write down every error, every comp drink, and every waste item to show where this liquor is going. It is your job to make sure the bar is showing a profit when the numbers are crunched. Where the owner typically makes a higher profit percentage is on the draught beers and well liquors. Each of these items is typically marked up 600–1000%. However, the money being made is on the name brand items, not because of the percentage, but because of the dollar amount.

Where does this money go? When you own a business, there is a large amount of overhead that needs to be paid. In any business, you must carry insurance, worker's compensation, and many other types of bills to be legitimate in your dealings with Uncle Sam. When you own a bar, for instance, the insurance that you have to carry is very costly. You must have this insurance to have a liquor license—another expense that is accrued by the owner. Plus, he must pay your wages. Remember earlier in the book when I said that you should get paid what your worth? Well, if all bartenders understood the amount of money the owner had to make to stay in business, there would be less stealing in this business. If you are able to help the owner by being trustworthy, that would be half the battle. You have every right to ask for a raise if you are doing the right things for the bar owner. The way to do this is by always being in charge and think of yourself as the owner. This will ensure that you will do what's best for the establishment and the customers at all times. If every bartender in the establishment had this frame of mind, you would have yourself a very well run bar.

If you have ever done the books for any type of business, you have heard of the Profit and Loss Statement. For most retail type businesses, it's good to have these done by your accountant at least on a monthly basis. Most bars that have a good working crew have a 12%–20% loss, or waste, average. That's pretty amazing when you think about it. For every four drinks that you sell, you dump another one down the drain. Or if you like to think of it as money, you only see four dollars of every five dollars that you should see coming in. That's why it's important to keep track of everything. Even in the morning when you have to pour half of a pitcher of draft beer for each type you serve, to get rid of the beer that's been in the line all night, or the ¾ bottle of red wine that you had to dump because it went bad. Both of these are considered a spill and should be written down on the spill sheet.

Some bar owners will give you the okay to have the house buy a regular customer a drink on occasion. That is where the Comp Sheet comes in play. Always mark down who the bartender was that gave the drink away and the reason why it was given away. This is a good way to cover your behind when someone needs to see where the liquor went when they are measuring the bottles.

As you can see, it is not all fun and games when you are slinging drinks. There are many responsibilities that you acquire once you step behind the bar. Yes, it is a fun and entertaining business as you will see. But, always take ownership of the establishment, so you do the right things. It will make your stay in this line of work a lot less stressful and more fun in the long run. As Murphy Law states: "When you least expect the worst to happen—it will." To be prepared, you must have control of your surroundings. Look at yourself as a juggler. All it takes for you to lose concentration is to drop one. Once you lose one, the rest will drop as well. Always, always be in charge of your surroundings and the rest will fall into place.

A little tip: If you are the one pricing the liquor, price it as if you are only pouring twenty five shots instead of thirty, (this pertains to liter bottles which contain 32 ounces of liquor. As you can see, two shots are usually given to you for error already). This gives you a little leeway when the final numbers are tallied. It also gives you a 1/4 shot of forgiveness for every drink you pour, so there will be no excuse for losing money at the end of the month. See the section "Pour a Good Drink" for a closer view of this.

3. EVERYONE IS YOUR BUDDY

This is the ultimate sin for any bartender and my number one pet peeve. When I go into an establishment to enjoy a few cold ones, the one thing I cannot and should not have to tolerate is waiting for a drink while the bartender leans down at the other end of the bar, talking to his friends that came in to see him at work. I don't know if it seems to be a growing problem because I'm getting old and have less patience, or whether most bartenders out there no longer care about serving the customer. Each and every one of us, in this business, needs to be aware of this ever growing problem. DO NOT NEGLECT YOUR CUSTOMERS! You need their business to survive. Every single person that is in front of you are just as important, if not more, than the friends who will come in to see you. In fact, your patrons should be treated like the friends that you have made outside the place you work. That is what will make you an above average bartender—the people who will come in to see you at your establishment. I am not talking about the friends who come in to see you, but the friends who you have made from the establishment which you are working. This is how you can tell a good bartender from an average bartender—the type of crowd that they attract.

This, above all the other rules, seems to be the hardest to comprehend with the new generation of bartenders out there. The attentive bartender will always have a following that every person in the occupation can only dream of having. Guess what? If you follow this rule, you WILL have the type of clientele that you want to have in your establishment. In fact, you have the total say on who will and who will not be a regular at your bar. You are, more or less, hand picking the type of crowd you want to have at your place, without the knowledge of the customers, of course.

Keep this in mind: If a person wanted to go to a bar just to have a drink, don't you think that they would have made it a cheaper night by going to the convenient store and picking up a six pack, before going home to catch up on some TV? There are exceptions to the rule, as in all other rules. However, your typical patron wants to come in for a little camaraderie. They want to come in and know that they have someone to talk shop to, or to talk about last night's baseball game. If this patron happens to be coming in to see you, they have included you in their circle of friends. They have come in to see how you are doing and to take the edge off of a very long day at work. As their bartender, you should feel the same about the individual as he does you. Look at it as someone coming over to hang out at your house. Remember: take ownership of the room. This IS your house! Make this customer feel welcome by giving him some good conversation.

Let's go back to the "outside of work" friends that drop by to see you at your place of employment. Whenever someone I personally know comes in to see me while I'm tending bar, they have already been prepared, by me, and that they would be treated no better than the people that come in and frequent the seats of the establishment. In fact I have been told by my friends, on a few occasions that I tend to ignore them when they come in while I'm on the other side. I doubt this to be true. They probably assumed that I would devote more time to hang out with them since they took the time to come and see me. To put this in to perspective, how would your friend feel if you were to go into his work and try talking with them when they had other things to do? Sure, it will be good to see this person to take a little break from the day. However, there are things that you are responsible for, and you must tend to these to ensure the day to move smoothly. Believe me when I say that your friends will understand. If you are good at your trade, they will just enjoy watching you at your craft.

One point of being a friend to the people that hang out at your establishment is that friends introduce other friends to one another. The thing that will keep everyone comfortable at the bar and wanting to come back is to make sure the regulars know each other. I make it a point to introduce total strangers sitting to each other at the bar, especially if the two are on their own. As I said earlier, the rule is that they are there to be social. This is the rule nine out of ten times. This is the main reason why people pay the money they do when they go out to the bar. They do not want to be stuck home all alone. Introducing your crowd to one another also creates a comfortable, friendly atmosphere in your bar. This concept reminds me of the whole "Cheers" perspective of "a place where everybody knows your name."

Seeing IS believing. The next time you are behind the bar give this a try: Purposely talk to a couple of people that are total strangers to each other at the bar. You can start by getting into an innocent conversation about sports, or some other common topic, with only one of the people—preferably someone that you have some history with. See how the one at the next barstool is reacting to the conversation and begin talking as if they are in the middle of it. Once you see them beginning to have some interest, ask them their comments on the topic. That's when you have snared them in your web. Proceed with the conversation by introducing the two parties to each other. When you feel that you have done your part, move on to take care of the other customers. When you glance down to see how the two parties are doing without you there, you will notice on most occasions that they have started on another conversation. These types of introductions three or four times per shift and you are building your crowd—your clientele. Once you have this concept down, you will be amazed how many of these folks will come back on that same night to have more conversations with the other people that they have met at the bar.

Another good rule of thumb, especially if you are working in a place that is somewhat larger, is to make the bar one big happy party. You are creating an atmosphere that will bring people back in that want to be part of it. Customers will feel that they have achieved social status at the bar and you, their bartender, have become one of their allies. All people want to feel that they belong somewhere. Humans are social creatures by nature. If you put them in a place where they are welcomed and feel they belong, then you will have a customer for life.

It's a fulfilling experience when you begin to see your business getting busier. This is the beginning of a process; a process that you should continue until the day you are no longer in the business. Try to be friends with everyone at your bar. If you doubt this will work, prove me wrong, and give it a try. Of course, you will have to build a rapport at the beginning for this to be successful. This should not be a problem, since you should be doing this with every individual that enters your door.

Keeping the above concept in mind, I would like to share a true example on how this rule played out for me. For the bar that I will be talking about—it not only made more money in tips for me—it saved the business altogether:

I was coming back from trying to make Key West my permanent home. After realizing that this lifestyle would probably be the end of me, I decided to make it a short stay. So I didn't have to hunt for a job when I got back home, I began to call some of the bar owners that I knew on my long drive back to Ohio.

I called a guy who was a regular of mine when I tended bar in Downtown Akron. When I was working there, he had the best restaurant/bar down the road, and would occasionally pop in to wet his whistle. He was known for his great business mind in the industry and was always successful in his ventures. Surely, he would have something for me or know someone that was looking for an experienced bartender. Before I left for paradise, I heard that he had opened up a small deli with a bar on the outer suburbs. I wanted to see how that was doing, as well. I had not seen him in a couple of years and was hoping to see that he was still doing well in the business.

I was kind of surprised when he told me that they were having problems getting people to patronize his place. This building that he opened up in was in a prime spot. It was the where most of the high rollers resided and there was nothing near by. However, this was originally a gas station and was not very big. His place had originally opened as just a deli to serve take out customers for lunch.

He put a bar in it to bring more people to dine in. He asked me to come to see him when I got back in town.

I didn't know what to expect when I walked in. The bar had been in place for a good year and they still had not established a dine-in clientele. The restaurant consisted of only ten tables. With the amount of people coming in to eat, they didn't even need one. The bar, consisting of fifteen barstools, made up half the space for the front of the house. It was a beautiful setup. I felt that once they started coming in, they wouldn't stop. He asked if I felt that I could turn this around for him. I told him to give me a few months and he would need to build a bigger building.

What was nice about coming into this was that I had worked five miles in either direction and had built up a good clientele in these establishments. All I had to do to start bringing people in was to tell my clientele that I was back and to come down and see me. This would give us the bodies to start bringing more people in.

The neighborhood was one in which no one knew each other. Unless you had kids playing in sports or you were involved in community politics, it was more than likely that a person would not know their neighbor. I would have to give the people that would come in a reason to come back. When I was lucky enough to have two people sitting at the bar, I would introduce them. I began to notice, by the third week, that these same people were coming in to talk to one another. They would occasionally bring in others to check out their new watering hole. Then I would introduce more. By the end of the third month, we would have every table and barstool filled with people eating lunch and supper. We also started doing a killer happy hour, with no less than twenty people standing in the aisles, waiting for a stool to open. It became the place to socially meet and be seen in the community.

It did not hurt us one bit that the food in this place is out of this world. The Akron and Cleveland papers, hearing about our popularity, came in and did stories on us. After that, it normally would take an hour for you to get a seat during the dinner rush. All of this happened in a matter of six months. It is still busy to this day. One year ago, they celebrated their tenth anniversary.

One thing to keep in mind is that you, as a bartender, are just a part of the big picture. However, it is up to you to have the personality it takes to get the crowd to start coming in. I feel that without this beginning push, this place would have failed. They went from only bringing in $300 a day in sales, (mostly takeout orders), to generating over $5000 a day. And we are talking about a place that used to be a Marathon gas station—a very small place. But, it has that one thing that a lot of other places lack. It has the atmosphere that everyone wants to be part of.

To this day, I would have to say that this place was my biggest accomplishment in the bar business. This was my last full time gig as a bartender. I still work in the business, but only on a part time basis, due to me starting a family. But I still, to this day, find my car veering in the direction of this place to say hi to all of the friends that I made in this fine establishment. With one of the bartenders, that I had the honor of working with now the man in charge, I know that the bar is in good hands.

This is how to build a customer base at every bar. It could take a good four to six weeks to see things begin to take shape. But, once you start to see it happening, you will be experiencing the first stages of having your very own "following". The most beautiful parts of the crowd coming in are what come with it: A larger increase in your tip jar at the end of your shift and the feeling of accomplishment every time you end your day at the job.

Every profession involves some sales to build up the business. The bartender is the salesman for any establishment in which he or she works. You must sell the atmosphere and the products to ensure that the customer will come back a second time. If the person you are serving feels unappreciated, they will go elsewhere. If they feel unwanted, they will never step foot in your place again. Your job is to make sure that they know that they will enjoy every minute that they are there. To do this, the most important part of the selling process is selling the customer on YOU.

If you follow this rule, you will be on the fast track of being a "bartender" and not just that average Joe filling drink orders, looking at the clock, anxiously waiting for their shift to end. On top of the friends that you already have, you will have a group that will come in to see you that you can call "your clientele". This sure makes this feel a lot less like work and more like a night out with your buddies.

4. BE A GOOD LISTENER

There are days that all you want is to know that everyone in your establishment is in total bliss, mingling, and breathing in the atmosphere. You have completely fulfilled their craving for a good time, good eats and some fine drink. Then you look down the bar and notice the one person, who always seems to have a smile on their face, looking like they need someone to talk to. In this line of business, we are the ones who sit there and take the good with the bad with our customers; the friends that we have acquainted ourselves with. This is where our job and wit is tested. You need to understand that there will be days where everyone will not be in the right frame of mind. It is our job—our duty as the server of people—to be there to listen. This is a job of being that friend that this person is hoping that you have become to them.

We, as human beings, have our bad days. The worse thing that you can do is to bottle these up until you are about to explode. You want to have that one person that is willing to listen, just to listen, so you can just get this weight off of your chest. Knowing that you have that person taking in every word will release the inner thoughts that you felt you could never share. That is all that someone else needs sometimes—that lending ear. Someone that you know will feel no less of you than before you told them your story.

We are the happy face that everyone that visits grows to trust. If we do our jobs to the fullest, we have become someone that our customers know they can talk to when they need to get something out in the open. They can do this knowing that it is our little secret; something that will not be shared with anyone else. This is part of the job. This is part of being a good friend.

This next story is very light in comparison to some of the others that I have in my memory banks. However, I don't think my friend will mind me telling this one. The others that come to mind, as promised by me at the time, will never be shared with anyone else. To those of you that have told me these stories, you can rest easy knowing that the stories shared will go with me to the grave. You have my word as a friend.

It was a Sunday afternoon and I had just come on duty. As I would typically do when relieving the daytime bartender; I went around and said hi to all of the customers. When getting down to one of the people at the corner of the bar, I noticed that this always happy individual seemed very sad. She tried to hide the fact that she was feeling this way, but this had overcome her to the point where the poker face wasn't going to fool me. As any bartender should, I went about my business setting things up and getting ready for my shift. I figured that she would let me know what was troubling her if she wanted to. I had known this person for a long time and knew that she would eventually break her silence and tell me what ailed her. However, it is not my place to open a can of worms. Always allow the customer to do this on their own free will.

After getting finished with my duties, I went over to tell my friend, I will call her Casey, about this funny thing that happened to me on the way to work. If I couldn't get her to spill the beans, I was going to make her forget about it by making her laugh. I didn't finish the first sentence when she began crying. "I had to put my dog down," she whimpered. "I have had her for twelve years—since being on my own. I don't know what I'm going to do." I listened intently while she talked about her best friend, and all of the things that they used to do together. She had lost someone that had become part of her. A piece of her had died. Casey had come from her mother's house where she had spent the last couple of days. She had not been home since taking her dog to the vet. She was afraid that she would feel even worse if she did. Looking like she hadn't gotten any sleep in those two days away from home, I finally convinced her that she should go home and get some rest. I happened to have the next day off. After a little coaxing, I insisted I would pick her up for dinner after she got off of work. There was a new place in the valley that I wanted to try and I hated to eat alone. This, I told her, would get her mind off of her loss for a couple of hours.

The next day, as promised, I picked my friend up to enjoy a few hours out of the house to treat her to the new restaurant in town. I asked her if she would mind if we made a quick stop to, my friend, Jim's house to drop off a guitar that he forgot at my house a few nights earlier. As we pulled up to his house, he waved us into his garage.

Knowing that Jim's cocker spaniel was about to give birth to a litter of puppies, I had called him earlier in the day to ask when she was due to give birth. "They were born a couple of days ago. Why do you ask?' That's when I told him the story about Casey's loss. "If she doesn't mind having a mixed breed, bring her over.' I got a very strange look from him when I handed my guitar to him as we entered the garage.

As I was introducing him to Casey, he led us over to the far back corner of the garage where his dog was nursing her new litter of four puppies. "Casey, Shaun told me your story," he said. "Please, take a pick of the one you want and you can come back and get her when she's old enough." With the look that I got from Casey at that moment, I was afraid that I had stepped over the line. I didn't know if I had made a smart move. "Let me think this over", she returned.

As we were driving to the restaurant, there was about a minute of awkward silence, which at the time seemed a lot longer. I finally came out and apologized for assuming that she would want another companion so soon after her loss. I told her that I could get a hold of Jim later if she changed her mind. "Oh, I don't need to change my mind about anything", she grinned. "I'm having a hard time deciding which one I want. Thanks for doing that. That's something I didn't think would happen today."

After a fine dinner and some good conversation, we went back to Jim's so Casey could make her selection. I have lost contact with her through the years. But, I hope that she and her new companion are sharing many years of joy together.

We as bartenders have to be there and give support to the people who come and visit us at our bar. That story, as I stated earlier, is very light in comparison to the ones that I have heard throughout the years in this business. I want to believe that I have saved some lives in some of the conversations I have had with my customers. We all have the human trait going for us in which bad days will come around every once in a while. It's always good to know that we all have someone to talk to when ever those days show their ugly head. We are there as the person they can talk to who will be neutral—someone who has no reason judging the person telling the story either way. They just want someone who will listen and maybe throw in their two cents without any prejudice.

We all have those demons and we need to vent those to feel somewhat normal on occasion. All it will take is as little as a dollar for a soda to go in to get some things out of your system, by just being able to tell another person. So, come take a seat and tell us what ails you if you feel the need. We are always there to listen.

Warning: It is important to remember who we are and who we are not when we are being good listeners. If you feel that an individual needs more help than what you can give them, you may want to give them the advice to seek professional counseling. You may find yourself saying something wrong that would trigger someone going into a tailspin. Keep within your bounds and be careful on who you give advice to. Yes, you are there to be a friend. But you will never be a cure-all to everyone's life issues.

5. POUR A GOOD DRINK

Everyone that has decided to open and read the pages of this book knows that this is one of the rules to be an above average bartender. However, my definition of this rule is not what you think when I am talking about pouring a good drink. Mixing a drink, in itself, is an art form that must be mastered when working in this occupation. There are reasons why there are books of recipes. One must know not only what goes in the drink; they must know what it takes to prepare the drink properly. This, as well as the previous things discussed in the book, does take time to accomplish. You must first be willing to learn the trade by seeing the experienced bartender doing it first hand. That's why it is good not to rush too quickly to take your spot behind the bar. There are certain things you will learn that a book will never be able to teach you. How much is too much when shaking a beverage? When should you stir and not shake? What types of garnishes go into certain drinks? What liquors should never be mixed together? The questions can go on and, quite frankly, we are going to go off the path that will lead us in the direction I want to go in this book. We will go into more specifics in another volume.

You will be serving different types of people with different tastes. Some will come up to you and be very straight forward in telling you they want a heavy pour. Others will ask for a taller glass so they won't taste the booze. No matter what the customer wants, you should begin their first beverage by pouring what the recipe calls for. Once you have the opinion from the customer on that first drink, you can add or subtract counts of juice or liquor to meet their satisfaction. This, of course, should always be done in moderation. You are there to not only measure for inventory purposes; you are there to measure the amount of liquor the customer is consuming. You and the customer will be able to keep better tabs of consumption. Law recognizes one ounce of liquor as being a serving. You must keep an eye on the customer's tolerances to ensure their safety, as well as those that will be around him or her during their time out. This includes a safe ride home—not only for them, but with the people that will be driving at that time as well.

If you have several people that come in on a frequent basis that ask for more than what is called for in terms of liquor, you can find yourself on the short side when inventory is done. Those little extra splashes, you feel are not noticeable, will add up quickly. You must do things to give yourself the confidence you need to not only keep the customers happy, but the owners of the establishment knowing that you are not shorting them at the end of the day. The following are some methods to give you a leg up. First of all, make sure you check the liquor laws in your state before following any of these guidelines. The last thing you need is any legal problem due to not following the rules. We have gone through a few of these earlier in the book. The rules previously looked at in the book go hand in hand with what is now being discussed.

MEASURES TO KEEP YOUR INVENTORY IN CHECK:

1. When you know you will be pouring "stiff" drinks for a couple of regular customers, keep a log and speak with the owner. There are thirty two shots, (thirty two ounces), of liquor in a liter bottle. This is the most common size behind the bar, or should be. Most bars recognize a liter as only having thirty shots of liquor, already giving you a two ounce leeway. To give you even more room for error, it is a good idea to have the bottle looked at as having twenty five shots of liquor, when pricing, and then price the shots according to that scale. Most states tax the amount of bottles bought and inventory. If you are in charge of keeping prices where they need to be to satisfy the owner, discuss this with him. He will appreciate the idea.

2. For the boss's records and to cover your own bases, it is always a good idea to make up a Spill Sheet and Comp Sheet behind the bar. All bar owners and managers like to know where the inventory is going—even if it is down the drain, so to speak. As discussed earlier, you must have traceability of your liquor. This will keep the owner aware of the situation and will give him the confidence in knowing that he has someone that is working at keeping his bar a profitable establishment. There is one downside to having too much on these sheets: you will have to raise prices to compensate for spilling or giving too much of your inventory away. These sheets will keep you more aware and more careful not to overdo it in either circumstance.

3. The oldest bartender trick in the book: If you know a customer likes a "stiff" drink, pack the glass with as much ice as possible in a glass before pouring your regular shot. They will be happy to have the drink taste much stronger due to less space for mix.

4. Some folk may not want the amount of liquor that a drink calls for. They may prefer less booze due to flavor, or possibly just keeping themselves in line. They know their limits and what they can tolerate. If this is the case, by all means, give them what they want. You will be further ahead in the long run.

5. Another idea, which may not be the best advice but can be used on occasion. When a customer orders a frozen, fruity drink, the amount of alcohol specified in the recipe is not exactly necessary. You will be giving them an ample amount of sugar and fruit in the drink on top of the booze. People generally order the drinks for the sweetness of the drink and to hide the flavor of alcohol in the beverage. So, feel free to skim back on the amount of alcohol; but not to the point that they aren't getting what they paid for.

If you are going to go either way to strengthen or weaken a drink—never go more than 1/8 of an ounce either way. If you happen to be adding more than that to a drink, offer the customer the option of getting a "double". That way you will be charging them for their tastes. You will then be controlling the inventory and giving the owner of the establishment the profits he is expecting, and peace of mind knowing that he has someone working who has the establishment's best interest in mind at all times.

Stiff—There are two meanings of this word in the bar and restaurant industry. The one referred to in this section is a strong drink; one with more booze than what is normally poured in that specific drink. The second definition is when you are not given the tip money you usually get for a specified amount on a bill. Example: "That guy stiffed me. I only got two dollars tip on that forty dollar check".

A double—When one shot of liquor is not enough, and the customer wants double of what is normal in a specific drink; two shots of liquor instead of one. Example: "Give me a vodka and tonic—and make it a double."

6. KNOW YOUR CUSTOMERS' DRINKS

I am a true fan to the bartender who goes out of his or her way to remember the drink, and the proper preparation of that drink, for the customer who has been into their establishment more than once. As I have said previously, and will probably say several more times, the customer wants to feel as though they belong in your establishment. It is up to you to make the customer feel that they are wanted and that you appreciate their business immensely. This rule will put the exclamation point on this feeling. Just the fact that you have remembered something about them makes them feel warm and fuzzy inside. You have accomplished your goal. You have gained a client who will frequent your business more than if you would not have remembered his drink. If you are married, you will understand this. You know what your wife's favorite food, drink, and movie are—don't you? If not, you may want to find out before she decides to knock you to the curb! Remember: your customers are the most important factor of your job! Before they get that feeling that you will never know who they are—or care for that matter—you might want to work on finding ways to remember this vital information.

I have learned through the years that this is the way to go. Not for only the satisfaction of the patron you have gained, but also for the time factor. When a customer, that regulars your establishment, walks in—it only takes a nod from them to know that they will be having the "usual". This will make your life much easier and keep you more in sync with the others at the bar. It takes about thirty seconds to say your hellos, and ask someone what they are having, when you don't have this knowledge. Sure, you will have some customers that will have something different every time they come in. But most will have the same drink as they always do. Make it a personal challenge to be good at this. You will gain time and more customers if you are.

There are times when this rule should never be used. This is usually when someone that frequents your bar comes in and does not give you the nod, or he walks in with a group unfamiliar to you and the establishment. Your customer may be with some people and doesn't want them to know how "regular" a customer he may be. He may be with a group of business associates he is taking out for dinner, or he may be with his in-laws. Either way, it may be a bad thing to jump the gun and act like he is there every day. ALWAYS make sure to catch their eye and get the high sign to know when the coast is clear.

My biggest fault is not remembering people's names. This one rule, I feel, is a major reason for this. I have concentrated so much on remembering my customer's drinks that I either forget to ask their name or just forgot it altogether. Do not forget to ask what their name is when you first make them a customer. I had an embarrassing situation happen to me at a cook out one day. My wife and I were invited to go to this all day affair. Another guest at the party happened to be a good customer of mine at the bar. I only knew him as his drink. He always had a certain draught beer with a warm glass and a twist of orange he would like rubbed on the rim and dropped in the beer before I served it. It was embarrassing when he came up and wanted an introduction to my wife. I could not, for the life of me, remember his name! Try to make a habit of remembering the name of the person with the drink—not just the face of the person with the drink.

The general rule when trying to remember a person's name is to repeat it five times in a conversation with them. You will be more apt at remembering it subconsciously the next time that you see them. The same rule comes to play when remembering someone's drink. Of course, you will not repeat it five times to the customer that you are serving. This will only seem redundant to the person you are serving the drink to. However, I have a good way that you can repeat it five times without looking like a buffoon. I encourage you to do this with every new person that enters your establishment. You will be overly amazed at the results.

1. When a customer orders a drink, repeat it to them as it was ordered.

2. Say it to yourself as you prepare to make the drink.

3. Say it to yourself as you are making it.

4. Say it to yourself when you are starting their tab.

5. Repeat saying it to the customer when you serve it to them.

As you can see, you are only orally saying it to the customer two times. This is more than enough as far as they are concerned. When you are saying to them on the second occasion, at the time you are placing the drink in front of them, you have let them know that it was what they had called for in the first place.

7. PROMOTE, PROMOTE, PROMOTE

This is one of my favorites on the list, and a great aspect of being in the bar world is the ability to self-promote so freely. You must do this to establish new clientele at your bar, and in order to do so you have to promote at other bars and social gatherings. At these other establishments, you are able to see how the clientele behaves in this environment first hand prior to them stepping foot into your place of business. You can filter out the good with the bad beforehand, which will save you the aggravation down the road. Also, it gives you a legitimate excuse to go out for a couple of drinks and mingle in places other than the bar you work at.

There is a second benefit to visiting other establishments on your off time. You can do comparisons on your business and theirs and ensure that you are doing some of the right things when drawing people in. How do you know if your place is doing above par if you don't check out the place down the road every once in a while and compare? We will go more into that in the next rule.

A good way to promote your establishment is to have food specials on particular nights. To make these nights public knowledge, it is good to advertise in newspapers and radio so you can attract new people. You should keep these specials going for long stretches, so people can get used to making that their weekly dinner stop. At one place that I worked, we had daily happy hour specials. On Monday, you could come in and enjoy shrimp cocktail for 25 cents apiece. On Tuesday, enjoy wings with your favorite sauce for 25 cents apiece, or come in Wednesday for our 25 cent apiece Mussels. This establishment has been doing this for years and hasn't changed a thing. This is why they are busy at this time every night of the week. They have people accustomed to coming in on particular nights for their favorite food for a fraction of the cost. It took awhile to build the business to the point of satisfaction. But, once they did, they have had standing room only success. Though it may take time to build your business, it is important to stick to your guns. Never give up on these specials. If you change things too often, people will never know what's coming. They will go where they know what they will be getting.

Something I would do to bring the late night crowd was to establish food specials from 10pm to midnight. We would have certain nights for shrimp cocktail, wings, and also had a cheap steak dinner once a week. Of course, to keep everyone happy, we would have our free chips and salsa after midnight, so even those last call customers could have something to nibble on. These later than most crowds would typically be some restaurant and bar people in the area just getting off from work. You are almost assured the best tips at the end of the night by putting some munchies out for the folks who make a living in the same industry as you. Plus, more times than not, they will bring some of their own clientele in for these late night feed fests.

Depending on the type of bar you are working at, there are various ways to promote yourself and the establishment for which you are employed. This cannot be said enough: YOU are the person who brings the people into your establishment; YOU are the one who decides what type of clientele will frequent the bar; YOU are the one who establishes the type of money you will be making by the amount of tips you will be receiving from your happy clientele. Part of the purpose of using different methods of promoting is that you will attract different people in with these various methods. You must use the right promotions to fit the type of environment for which you work. Some things work great for one place and will not work well in others. This is another thing you must use trial and error on to ensure success. However, you must also keep this rule of thumb when you are promoting the bar—don't be too quick to judge if something is or isn't working. As in anything in life, you have to give your idea a fighting chance to prove itself. If you don't, you have less chance of success and a greater chance of failure. You must have patience. Give it a good few months before dropping it and moving on to something else.

Some methods of promotion are listed below. Don't stick with only one promotion. The more you promote your bar, the greater the chance of success. You have to give a little to get a little in this line of work. Always discuss your ideas with the owner or manager before trying them out.

IDEAS TO PROMOTE YOUR ESTABLISHMENT

1. Have specials on different types of appetizers on a given night. Try it when drink specials are also present, like happy hour for instance. This will give the people getting off work something to nibble on while winding down with their favorite beverage. Wine specials, with a nightly special entrée, are a good way to ramp up on liquor sales during the dinner rush.

2. Happy hour drink specials, to go along with those appetizer specials, are the most popular of most bars. This is because they always work. Make sure to make your happy hour better than what the competition is offering down the road. People who frequent the happy hour time are usually looking for the best deals.

3. Promote dart and pool leagues. This can only be done if your establishment has the room to have the proper equipment for these types of leagues. People from different bars will come in on various nights of the week to compete with your home team. The only downside to this is that your team will have to travel to the other bars on some nights. Be sure to compensate the traveling nights with some open pool and dart tournaments to get the interest from the other clientele in the establishment.

4. Karaoke nights are a great source of entertainment. This is especially true for those who have had a little too much to drink and have the liquid courage to go up and sing some Old Blue Eyes. This type of entertainment will draw people in that would otherwise never step foot into your establishment. However, there are people that can't stand to listen to juiced up people singing badly. But, if you keep this a set time once a week, these folks will know when to find something else with their time, and you can attract a different clientele for this once per week entertainment.

5. Live entertainment is an excellent way to bring people into your establishment. But be sure that the band you are bringing in has a good following, and are good in the first place, or you may find yourself with fewer patrons than you started with. A musician friend of mine started an "Open Mike Night" at a bar several years ago to help bring customers in on an otherwise slow time of the week for this establishment. Open Mike Night is where you have a house band warm up and have other musicians come in with their instruments. They would then take turns going up and performing various cover songs. By the end of the night, they would have a pretty good Jam Session going on. This bar is so busy now on this particular night, that it does more sales than any given Friday or Saturday night.

6. Sponsoring various sports leagues, such as bowling, softball, volleyball, etc, is a great way to bring in some loyal customers. I would always make it a point to let them know that the cost of sponsoring their team required them to come down and have a couple of drinks after their games. It wasn't uncommon to have more than just the teams coming in. They would usually bring some of their audience with them when the game was over. It helps to have some appetizer specials available to these customers, so they will be more apt to dine in. This will give you a better bill average, meaning a higher tip. There is another important factor in this type of promoting. It shows the

neighborhood that you are there to be a supporting factor for the community, and not just another bar.

7. With permission from the management, get some personal business cards made up with your name and title. On the back of the card, have an enticement to come into the bar, such as a percentage off food or a free appetizer with any entrée order. Not only does this type of promoting get your name out there; it also gives your place of business a presence outside of the four walls of your establishment. People are more tempted to come in to your place if you are willing to give them an incentive.

There are several other ways to promote your establishment. I will leave the rest to your imagination.

You will get what you put into it when it comes to promoting. It's all about the way you sell the establishment. There are times when you may have an idea that you have never seen done before. There are four things to ask yourself when you are putting together something new in terms of promoting your establishment:

- *What type of clientele am I trying to attract?*

- *What can I do that would be different than what everyone else is doing?*

- *How can I get the word out to people about the establishment with the least amount of money for advertising?*

- *Who do I need to talk to, besides the management, to make sure that what I am doing is in accordance to the liquor laws of the state in which I work?*

The first three questions are self explanatory. The forth is something you should do your homework on. As in any state I have worked in, there are many laws that are enacted by the liquor control boards that are in a gray area. Meaning: There will be one liquor authority that will tell you are in accordance with the law. Then you will have another tell you that what you are doing is not. When you talk to someone about the promotion that you want to do, make sure you get the name of the individual that you talked to and log the date and time. To make sure that your idea is within the law, it is not a bad idea to call and speak with another agent. That way, you have two names that you can fall back on if any questions arise.

8. KNOW YOUR COMPETITION

I could have probably put this as part of the "Promote" section, but it would have diminished the importance on the subject. This is the gauge that you will have to see how the types of people, which you want as clientele, feel about your establishment vs. the other establishments in the area. You should know where you stand as a place of business, and be able to critique the areas you need to improve, to be the best. The only way to do this is to know your competition.

Now, when I say competition I don't mean enemy! In the bar industry, there is no such thing as bad competition. Unless of course, the other bar is looking for ways to thin out your herd, (patrons), and put you out of business. This would not be a good thing for us or for him for that matter. That's because all restaurant and bars feed off of each other. That is the reason you see several eateries/bars within a miles radius of each other. Like it or not, you will not be the choice of all people when it comes to places to hang out. You must find your own niche to satisfy the few that do decide to enter your place of business. You will learn that if you work as a group, you can attract more people to that one area; to enjoy maybe your place for an appetizer and a drink, then off to the place down the road for an entrée before hitting the movie theatre. There are things that one place can take from another to better each other's establishments. This will gain more interest from more people to go to the area, making both establishments busier.

When I worked in Dallas, TX, I had the opportunity to work with one of the Bar/Restaurant Associations in the city. This is where the bar owners, executive chefs, and several bartenders would meet once a month to discuss current events within the industry. It was where people would share ideas that would not only better their place of business, but better the quality of every establishment in the area. This only creates more business being generated due to having more than one good stop in one region. People don't only want to go to one place—then home. Most people want to try out a couple of places. They will go where it will be more convenient to do just that. Many large metropolises have established this type of group. Not only do they share ideas; they keep everyone on the same page in terms of law changes that can either benefit or hinder the businesses in that particular region.

The major reason for such a brotherhood is due in large part to the many laws and regulations that have come about in the past twenty years. Bars need to find ways to draw people in. The "busy bar on every corner" age has passed us due to these new laws. People aren't apt to come in then drive home for the fear of getting a DUI. We must be more aware of what we need to do as a group, so we can all survive. Promoting shuttle services and free taxis is a good way to keep all of us thriving in our business. Promoting such services, as a group, will ensure that there will never only be one stop. It will also keep everyone, which has enjoyed too many pops, off of the road.

It is also good to know as many of the other bartenders in your region as possible. Other than knowing how he is doing compared to you, it is good to hang out with the people in the same field. That way, you can bounce ideas off of each other. Plus, you understand what this individual is going through when they say that they had a miserable day. These folks will be some of the only people getting off of work the same time you do, so it is hard not to hang out together. If you have some bar and restaurants that close earlier than you in your area, the best way to begin hanging out with them is to have them come to you.

I left this off of the Promote List on purpose. I felt that it fit better in this section. The best way to bring in other waiters and bartenders in your region, is to have a weekday night where there are discount prices for bar and restaurant employees. All they would need is proof that they work in an establishment so they can receive discounts on food, and possibly happy hour pricing for booze. These people will probably be your best customers. If you do everything you should to promote this night, you will end up making more money in tips in the three to four hours that they are there then you probably would for two of your regular full shifts.

Bringing in the competition is not hard if you have the right promotion. The hard part will be for you to have them continue to come in on a weekly basis. To have them become regulars will take the skills of an accomplished bartender. This group of people will want to be entertained and treated right. If you are not bringing them in regularly, you need to take a good hard look in the mirror, and fix this immediately. It will usually have something to do with the fact that you are not treating them as well as they feel they should be. Keep in mind that people who are in this business will be your biggest critics. They're also the individuals that will be the first to let you know what you need to do in order to keep them coming back—if you ask what it will take you to change for them to do so. Just be ready to leave your ego at the door if you're looking for some honest criticism.

If you happen to start working at a bar and you have a bar close to you that seems to be attracting the same clientele, there are ways to work with one another to have both places working to their fullest potentials. You might want to make your owner/manager aware of this other establishment, and give him ideas you have to attract some more potential customers to the area. Having the bars work together to attract more people will keep everyone happy and will benefit both establishments. Working together will make your area more than just a one stop region.

9. BE AN ENTERTAINER

We all have those days where you know you shouldn't even get out of bed. You feel like anything that you try to accomplish will turn out badly. You've got that, "Stay away from me or I may want to hurt you", feeling. Guess what? No one at your bar cares that you may be having a bad day. They may be there because their day has been no bed of roses either. They have come in to have their favorite bartender cheer them up. You have to put on that happy face that has brought them in so many times before. Being a bartender is like being on stage. You are there to perform and always be at your best. You are there to give your audience an uplifting experience, so they can forget about the day that they just had. Bartenders are paid to put on a show, no matter how bad their day has been. You are one bad day away from losing good customers and getting the hook from stage left. Keep your bad day where the coats go—closed up in the closet until you are out of there. One nice thing about changing into a good attitude when you get behind the bar is that it shows you that it was all in your mind that you were having a bad day in the first place. Just making yourself smile makes your bad day turn out to be okay, almost instantly, most of the time.

Entertaining your customers takes more than making sure they don't run dry. You have to have conversation. Part of your duties at the bar is to keep up with the box scores in all sports, know your current events, and know some off the wall trivia. This is a job where it is very beneficial to read a newspaper on a daily basis. It is always good to have a few new, fresh jokes to tell. Just make sure the audience on hand can stomach the one you are about to throw their way. Learning some basic bar tricks come in handy for those new folks that walk in from time to time. It definitely makes a great ice breaker.

My own favorite bartender, Alan, comes up with some off the wall trivial stuff that I always find intriguing. I will go in there just to hear one of his fascinating stories. One thing that he does on a yearly basis that I have always enjoyed, (this is a "can't miss" event in Akron, Ohio), is that he has a black tie affair during the Oscar's Celebration. This is your typical neighborhood bar, mind you! It's cool to go in there during this time to see people, who are your typical hard working Americans usually in their everyday garb, get dressed to the hilt for this joyous festivity. He hands out awards of his own for some of the outlandish things that have happened in his place throughout the year. Well, I am lucky enough to tell you that I have yet to receive one of these awards. I don't know if these festivities would be as fun if I was the brunt of it. But, it sure is a blast being part of the audience.

Entertaining at your bar could also mean being fancy with the bottle and glasses while making drinks. This is commonly known as "flair bartending". I am not a true fan of all of this nonsense. You tend to lose sight of the very reason you are back there in the first place: to serve the customer. I have been in too many places where I had to wait way too long for a drink, while the egomaniac behind the bar showed off his finesse. Don't get me wrong. There are times when you can do your show behind the bar. Just make sure that everyone that is there to drink has a drink in front of them before you begin this act. When I pick up glasses to make a drink, I will twirl it once in my hand to show off a little, or when I pick up empty beer bottles from the bar I will occasionally flip one behind my back before putting it into the garbage. However, you must always be aware of your time restraints. If you follow all of the rules of this book, you will not have the time to put on a five minute show. Keep everyone entertained by not entertaining too much when it comes to the flair.

Another reason why you should keep this type of entertainment to a minimum is that to err is human and you will have drops. What come with drops are breaks. When you're too busy and you don't have time to clean up your mess is the time that one of those drops will happen right over the ice! Do you know what happens when you break glass over ice? It makes every single cube in the ice bin contaminated. It will take you a good fifteen to twenty minutes to scoop out the ice … clean the bin out with a sanitized rag to make sure all of the glass chips are out … pour hot water to clear the drain … then go retrieve more ice to refill your ice bin. I think I've made my point.

Entertaining is much more than what you can do with a bottle. It has more to do with your attitude, your delivery on a joke, your telling a good story. It is someone who knows that they are there to be the one who will keep everyone on their toes; someone who will wait for the right time to tune in on a comment just for a laugh. Entertaining will keep everyone at your establishment happy. This will mean fewer fights due to disgruntled customers looking for something to occupy their time. Keep them busy by keeping them entertained. Your tip jar will fill up quicker if you can keep them smiling.

10. BE ETHICAL AND RESPONSIBLE

To be a great bartender takes all of the things that we have discussed to this point. However, you will have a very short stay in this business if you do not take this last rule to heart. You can skip and sidestep any of the other rules that we have mentioned except this one, if you want to make this a career. This is the one that will save you from being fined and, quite possibly, jailed. Following this rule will keep you from being black balled from the bartending industry, altogether.

There are many responsibilities you take on when you work at a place that serves liquor. You are handed these because the owner and manager feel that you can be trusted; you have done every other task that has been presented to you and you are ready for the responsibility. Let's go into some of these responsibilities in more detail.

There are laws in place that make the bartender and the bar that employs them responsible for the intoxication of the people that leave their establishment. This also holds true if you serve this person only one drink before realizing that he had been to other bars prior to yours. If they drive under the influence and get into an accident with another vehicle, kill either themselves or someone else in another vehicle, you can be found liable for the actions of that intoxicated person. As wrong as this may seem, it's something that is there and we have to except it. We have become a "sue—happy" society. People have a problem taking responsibility into their own hands and will use every resource to find someone else at fault for their own actions. For that very reason, it's important to keep an eye out for people who seem to have over indulged and have passed the realm of sobriety. Always, always, always make sure that someone who is not drunk will be driving them home. If they do not have a ride, call them a cab or have someone give them a ride home. I have had my fill of altercations with people who have fought me on taking their keys until the next day. However, most times they were the first to thank me the next time I saw them. You will be saving yourself a lot of grief later on by doing this.

One other major point is that of the money for which you will be handling while working behind the bar. When you are on your shift, it would be a perfect world if every one working had their own cash drawer, or bank, to use while they were there. However, if you already work behind a bar, you know that sometimes that is asking too much. You could have as many as four people ringing up bills and grabbing change from the same bank. This can become very confusing when you find yourself short at the end of the shift. That is why it's important to have everyone as responsible as the others when you have this happen. Make sure everyone counts the drawer before the shift begins. If you all came up with the same number, and you end up being short, everyone should pay up the difference in the drawer, by splitting up the loss.

One bad thing is that there are some people out there who have become pros at beating the system and learning how to steal by not ringing up food and drinks when they should have. That is where a good inventory comes into play. If you keep a good inventory, you will know if you are in line with what is being cashed in. Start with a weekly inventory. If things seem to be off kilter, and inventory is never meshing with the receipts at the end of the week, start taking an inventory every morning. That way, you can figure out where and what shift these shortages are occurring, and you won't be blaming the innocent parties.

If you happen to be a bartender who likes to pour heavy, please look back at the previous rules for an overview. Just because you're being generous doesn't make you a thief. However, it is important to remember that you are not at your house pouring a drink. This liquor belongs to this house and the owner who happens to have the liquor license. This is the only area where you need to understand that you are not the owner of the establishment. It is important to follow the rules on how to make the drinks. It's important to keep records of everything—to have traceability to cover your behind.

As much as I hate to say this, because this occupation is my passion; there are way too many bad seeds in this business. It only takes a few to make everyone else look bad. If you happen to work with someone who is doing some bad things, be sure to let the management know. This way they can cut their losses and get this individual out of there as soon as possible. Don't feel you are tattling or causing bad blood with the other co-workers. The person you are getting rid of only has themselves in mind. They wouldn't be doing it otherwise.

As in any profession, you must follow a Code of Ethics. That way, you will have no problem sleeping at night. You will have fulfilled the interests of not only the owner of the establishment, but also for the fellow workers who are there to work just as hard as you to ensure a nicely run establishment. Just follow the rules and you will surely benefit from it in the long run.

PART III
FIVE THINGS TO STEER AWAY FROM AS A BARTENDER

We have touched on a few of these topics briefly in the previous pages, but it's wise to cover these issues more extensively to give them their importance. In the world of bartending, you will learn that it is a balance of the yin and the yang. To give you full insight, we will dive head on into some of the things that are the "no nos" in this industry. You will learn that these things will always be present—tempting you to veer off the path in the right direction. So, it is important to have a better understanding as to why these things are not good and what you need to do to steer away from them.

I will be the first to admit that I have been at fault for not practicing what I preach on a few of these topics. It took many years of learning the hard way to see what can happen if you don't turn your cheek and ignore the temptations. These hard lessons made me realize that I needed to make some serious changes in order to be at the top of my game in this business. However, you will find yourself breaking some of these rules from time to time. To err is human, and sometimes that little voice inside our heads will take us away from what is sensible and wise. Sometimes, in the heat of the moment, we lose focus on what are the right ways to go about things. It will be up to you, during these lapses, to learn from your mistakes. You should be able to pick yourself back up and keep moving toward your goal—to be one of the very best and sought after people in the business.

Many aspects of this chapter are the reasons many choose this line of work in the first place. It is hard for anyone just getting into this business to comprehend how important these guidelines are to follow; how easily your reputation can be tainted. A bartender's reputation is vital to their career and takes time to establish. This is not something that you want to toss in the garbage for one night of fun and recklessness. As much as something seems to be okay to do at the time must be looked at a few times before moving forward. These things that we will be going over can, and will, ruin a career.

Take all of the sins that I present to you to heart. If you don't, you will have to work twice as hard, if not harder, to get yourself where you want to be.

1. DRINKING WHILE YOU WORK

Successful bartenders who have done their time in this industry will agree that this is a definite "DO NOT" rule. With the arsenal, (booze), always at arm's reach, it will always be a temptation to have a few with your friends while you work. You must constantly remind yourself that it can only take one shot to change your demeanor. This is never a good thing when you will have so much on your plate in this occupation. Feeling a buzz while you work can cause more problems than you want to get yourself into.

There are way too many responsibilities for you not to be in the right frame of mind when you are doing your job. One of these responsibilities is to make sure no one gets out of control at your establishment. You are there to be the anchor, the rock, so that everyone else can have a good time without worrying about having to handle someone that crossed the line from sobriety to all out drunkenness. With this in mind, how can you assume this responsibility when you have trouble keeping yourself in control? Who do you think will listen to a half intoxicated fool tell them that they have had too much to drink? Listening to someone in this state, as you will find out early in your career, will be something that will not happen. Remember—you must show self control and a well behaved demeanor when tending bar. You are there to be the example and the person who controls the environment. Without that control, you will not only lose good customers, you will lose respect from even the people who do lose control every once in a while. The bartender is there to ensure a good time is had by all. You must always be on your toes. The clientele are there to have a fun, yet still want a bartender that contains the establishment. Stay sober to give the clientele the sense of security and comfort they expect.

Another responsibility is keeping a balanced register. Drinking tends to impair quick thinking and slows your motor skills. For those of us who have over indulged on the other side, (guilty on a few occasions, yet learned my lesson), isn't it strange how the drawer never seems to be right at the end of the night? This is due, in large part, to not paying enough attention when giving people change. To make sure this doesn't happen, you must stay sober to keep your mind in the game. Not paying attention frequently can add up to many short money nights. This will get you ousted quickly by the management. That is, if the drinking doesn't cut your career short first.

Many night bartenders have the responsibility of locking up the bar at the end of the night. When the bartender has had too much to drink, they will either forget to lock the door or set an alarm. You might get lucky and no one will ever notice the error. But, chances are someone who out ranks you will be the one opening up the next morning. If they find the door being unlocked or the alarm not activated, you could find yourself in the unemployment line due to your lack of responsibility. Carelessness, in this business, is not acceptable—especially by the one who signs your paycheck. The insurance you have to carry in this business is VERY expensive. If you show a clean record, your insurance will be lower than that of the bar that tends to have workers who forget to do their duties and don't lock up correctly.

Another factor on the insurance: If the insurance company finds out the establishment was not locked properly and securely, (i.e. the drunken bartender forgot to secure the business before he went home), there is a better than good chance that they will not cover the losses that the business incurred. The bar could lose thousands of dollars because you felt the need to wet your whistle on one too many occasions this particular evening.

If you feel the need to drink while you are working, it is important to set yourself some guidelines, so you can stay focused on the most important part of your evening—your job. Keep a limit that you know won't hinder your performance behind the bar.

When working, I will keep my limit to two drinks. I usually will drink these at the end of the night, while everything is winding down. I stick to this limit. Do not find an excuse to have more because of some special occasion. If you find yourself doing so, look in the mirror to see if you might have a problem. When I say two I mean two—not two double shots with a beer chaser. Keep the way you make yourself drinks the same as you would your customer's: a true shot or true serving that makes one drink. This way, you are controlling your intake and ensuring you won't go overboard.

I can already hear the excuses you will have when you are behind the bar:

"When my customers buy me drinks, I feel obligated."
Customers are always going to buy you drinks. This is part of the territory. They see this as a gesture of gratification to you, as their bartender. However, who says you have to drink it at that specific time. Save the drink for later so you can enjoy it more. Most of your customers will understand and respect that.

I will always keep a sheet behind the bar to keep a tally of drinks that have been bought for me. At the end of my shift, I will cash in on a couple of these and take them off the sheet. It's nice to have this—especially on my off nights. This will give me an excuse to hang out with the people of this establishment and enjoy some time with them on their side. This will prevent me from having to spend my hard earned money on some spirits, by cashing in some chips that I had received through the week. Just be sure to take care of the person serving you those free drinks. They will be sure to return the favor one day.

If you sense that the customer is offended that you are not drinking what was bought for you right then and there, tell them your reasons for not drinking it at that time.

If they still seem upset, go more in depth with the rules that you have established for yourself while you are working. It should seem apparent, but they will respect you a lot more if you keep your cool and stay straight while you are serving them. After all of the above has been done and they are still upset, let them know when you will be getting off work. That way, they can come in at that time and buy you a drink. This will give you more time to sit around and shoot the breeze with that customer anyway.

You should never have any problem convincing your clientele that you don't like drinking while you work. These are YOUR customers and they have been brought in by you. If they do not understand, you can afford to lose them as a customer. They have not gotten that most important thing; why you are there in the first place. You are there to serve them and keep them safe.

"I can drink all I want and keep my composure."

Say what you want. Being a pro at drinking myself, I know it only takes one day for this theory to go out the window. I used to have this philosophy myself. When I was young, I felt that I had a full grasp of reality and thought I could drink everyone and anyone under the table. All it took was one night to change my outlook on that. Maybe I was feeling under the weather that day or had something in my system that didn't agree with what I was drinking. Whatever the case may have been, I was unable to finish my duties and wound up getting very sick, very quickly. Thankfully, another bartender was working this night and she took over my closing shift. I was even more fortunate that this individual didn't spill the beans and tell the owner.

It is very easy to become an alcoholic in this line of work—especially if you find yourself drinking on the job. Do yourself a big favor: as in any other job, drink only on your time off when all of your duties are complete. Even then you can find yourself getting too carried away. At the very least, you can find your time at work a time when you can stay sober and productive.

A buddy of mine, who I will call Steve, was probably the best all around bartender I had ever seen. He had this aura around him when he would enter a room. There was no doubt that, when he was present, the room was his. He always impressed me by the response he would get from the customers he was serving. This guy had no enemies; only friends that would come in and see him. If there was a picture next to the definition of bartender in the dictionary, it would be his. This man was possibly the greatest storyteller that I had the honor of listening to. I was in awe by the time he would finish telling his tales, real or fiction. I envied the fact that he would always seem to have everything under control. I worked with Steve a solid two years before realizing that he had a problem.

On a couple occasions, the bar manager approached me and inquired why we seemed to be going through a particular brand so quickly. The inventory verses the sales were not even coming close to matching up. I assumed that either a bartender had broken some bottles and forgot to write it on the spill sheet, or someone might have erred on the amount that we had when last doing inventory. One thing that I would have never imagined was that my best friend, the greatest bartender that I had ever seen, was over-indulging on a nightly basis. He did a great job of hiding it from all of us.

Things began to make more sense with the inventory one Friday night. As I was working alongside Steve, I happened to pick up his drink instead of mine. I was waiting to quench my thirst with the water that I had just poured for myself moments earlier. I took one big swig and thought I was going to spew all over the folks that were sitting in front of me. Boy, if you could have seen my reaction. It took me a good five minutes to regain my composure. Being his friend, I decided not to say anything to anybody about the incident. Maybe if I would have, he would still be doing something he was very good at. I guess I wasn't much of a friend after all.

It wasn't long after this incident that things started to become more obvious. He started showing up late for work frequently and started to act differently with everyone. I noticed that he was closing the bars he frequented every time he had a chance. He had gone over the edge. He was no longer able to control the drinking, and was not hiding his problem anymore.

One day, Steve got into a very bad car accident on his way home from work. He spent the next two weeks in the hospital. It was probably the best thing that could have ever happened to him. Once he got out, he decided to move back to where he grew up. From what I hear, he is now married with a couple of kids. I hope this made the difference in his life to get him off the juice.

The one thing to take from this story is that it is very easy to lose control of yourself when you drink behind the bar. You can lose everything that you have worked for if you can't say no to booze while you're serving it. Keep a straight mind, by staying straight behind the bar, and you will go far.

"I can only handle my customers if I'm drinking."

Well, this is a problem. There are a couple of reasons why someone may feel this way about their customers. The first of these is what I like to call "burnout". It is when you have this iron horse mentality when you start in the business. You tend to want to work as often as possible, so you can maximize your opportunity to make more money. What you will begin to eventually realize is that you start to either hate or feel sorry for the people who frequent the stools at your establishment. You reach a point where you no longer can tolerate the people in the bar. Another phrase for this is "overexposure to the drinking public." You begin to feel that drinking will ease these feelings a little. But, all you are really doing is putting an exclamation point on them. My advice to you is to cut down on the hours you are putting in so you can save your sanity.

I got out of working full time behind the bar because I quickly began to feel uneasy with the people I would serve. I would no longer have good conversation with them due to my burnout. You see, I had been working in the business since the age of twenty. The first ten years behind the bar I had become the work horse in every establishment that I was employed. I couldn't get enough of being on the other side. When I hit thirty, I became very pessimistic and edgy. I ended up being that regular guy serving drinks behind the bar, due to not wanting to talk to anyone.

I finally came to the conclusion that I wasn't giving myself enough "Shaun Time"—that time away from the every day grind to enjoy myself, and the things that I loved to do away from the bar. Soon after this, I dropped to only four shifts per week. My attitude eventually changed for the better and I was able to bring myself back to normal.

Then I learned something that I wish I had known all along—I was making more tips in those four days then I did when I was working myself into madness. This was all due to my mind set.

It's understandable how someone can drop off course due to a state of mind. Once you begin to feel this way, you have to find other alternatives besides picking up the bottle. Here are some tips to summarize this segment. Keep these in mind when you feel the urge to party on your employer's time:

1. Instead of working every waking hour to make more money, try to find ways to hone in on your skills in this profession. This will help you become a better bartender, so you can make more money to pay monthly bills and extra cash to do some fun things on your much deserved time off. All because you are in the right frame of mind at work.

2. Keep your shifts down to what you feel is tolerable. Do not live in the place you work. This will be what it seems when you work too many hours. This is one of the biggest downfalls for most people getting into this occupation. Burnout brings the worst out in people.

3. Try to limit yourself to only two drinks in your place of employment. If you feel like having more, find another place to hang out. Why would you want to stay at the place you just worked eight hours at? You will tend to hang out there more on your off time because you haven't given yourself time to meet people outside of the work place. It is never good to make the bar you work your favorite watering hole.

4. Instead of drinking after you get off work, find something that will be more constructive and beneficial for you. You will have more than enough time socializing with the customers while working. How about a round of golf or maybe a few frames at the nearest bowling alley? Explore an interest in art or literature, or spend some quality time at the gym.

5. Always bear in mind that bartending is your profession, your choice of a trade. If you remember this at all times, it will keep everything else in line.

Perhaps there's the chance that you are the type of person who doesn't like people in the first place, hence the reasoning for drinking while you work. Words of advice to those types: Get the hell out of this business!! You think you had trouble dealing with people before? Try tending bar for a little while longer. Soon you will find yourself in a fetal position, curled up under the bar with a bottle of whiskey in your hands.

2. RELATIONS WITH YOUR COWORKERS

Boy.... two hard ones in a row! By now you are thinking that I'm out of my mind, right? It's very hard to avoid this one when the temptation is always standing right in front of you. This wonderful person who you happen to work beside all day; they happen to share the same outgoing personality as you. It seems they want to know you better. They invite you to come over to listen to some good music on their new stereo system, while enjoying some after hour drinks and some good conversation. They coax you with a bottle of rum that they have just received from a friend who recently came back from a trip to Jamaica. Perhaps you have spent time outside of work with this individual. But, this time you will have the first opportunity to be alone, to go one-on-one. Your heart beats ten times its normal rate as you imagine the next couple of hours alone with this intoxicatingly beautiful human being. Before going any further with this fantasy, may I suggest?

DON'T DO IT!!!!

But, of course you'll argue, "Why shouldn't we do this? We get along great and always have fun with each other. Nothing will change that." That kind of mentality will only lead to disaster. Everyone knows that once you are involved with someone things do change. You can never go back to your innocent flirtations. The mystery, that has engulfed your curiosity for all this time, is now gone.

It's bad enough that we will occasionally grab some "victims" while serving someone who feels that curiosity with you. At least, they usually know what they are getting: a bartender that's looking for a good time. These customers typically have the same goal in mind. More often than not, it's usually the customers picking up the bartenders in the first place. But, doing this with someone you work with makes it different. Neither one of you can decide never to come back into the bar if this night of ecstasy doesn't match the fantasy. You will eventually have to work together again.

Once you engage in a fling with someone you work with, it will change the entire atmosphere of your work place. Even though both of you may declare that neither party wishes to get serious, you will both be on edge if something happens that makes the other person feel uncomfortable. Topics that you used to joke about with this person will now seem offensive to them. Wait until you have a chance to hook up with someone else at the bar, while the person you previously got together with is working right next to you. This kind of situation is never comfortable with either person. Unless, for some reason, they seem to be missing a soul, (I have encountered a few soul-less individuals in my travels), and could care less how you feel.

Sleeping with a coworker will forever change the way you react to each other. The change is not a good one in most of these cases. The worst aspect about any type of work relationship is that it involves you bringing your personal life with you to work. This is one of the deadliest sins of a bartender. You should never let your personal life come between you and what you want to create with your customers at your bar—the always easy going lifestyle that you are supposed to be living. Not many people have a good poker face when it comes to keeping a secret about sleeping with a coworker. I have always been amazed by how much people change their character with each other after one night of exotic bliss. Everyone at work *will* notice the change. You will begin to hear the rumors circling within the establishment about you and the other associate.

Once the damage has been done, there is only one feasible way to make everything right in the world again: One of you will have to find another job. It is the only way to reinstate any sense of normality in the work environment. The only plus side to this is that the rumors will stop spreading among the other coworkers and customers. Nobody likes it when coworkers talk behind their backs. This type of situation creates tension and sometimes that tension is projected onto the customer—which can be bad for business.

I also erred against this rule early in my career. It happened one night with a waitress that really knocked the breath right out of me. She was so stunning and beautiful; the room seemed to always be brighter and fuller of life when she was in it. "Bridget" would walk into a room and everyone would turn to watch her every move, including yours truly. Just to add to her physical presence was her over-glowing personality. This is a very bad mix when you are working with this type of individual. Every man and most women wanted the honor of even having a conversation with this girl. I was fortunate enough that she befriended me the first minute I arrived on the job. We became the best of friends and were inseparable. Everything between us was great until the night we went too far.

I have to explain the type of friendship we had in order for you to get the full spectrum of this story. We were always flirting with each other. It was the type of innocent flirting that would get to a point, and would abruptly stop. I came to enjoy these episodes during our shifts together. After I got past the initial physical attraction at the beginning of our friendship, I got to know the inner workings of this amazing woman. Being friends was more important to me than getting physical with her and damaging the bond we had created. I think this respect went both ways and I was content with that. Well, I accepted it anyway. I never thought in my wildest imagination that this fine looking creature would want anything more from me. I would soon discover that curiosity always gets the best of all of us, including with those fine looking girls.

One night, as the crowd began to wind down, I started pouring the drinks, which I had gotten orders on, for last call. Bridget was doing what she did best: gently turning down guys who had the courage to ask for her phone number. She came up to the bar for a break and asked me what I had planned after work. I told her I was thinking about hitting an after-hour party I had heard about earlier in the evening. I invited her to come with me, but she wanted to talk me into coming over to her place to watch some movies. Around this time in my life, I was not one to turn down partying with a friend in order to watch a movie and engage in some stimulating conversation. Bridget said she had rented a couple of comedy movies before work and had some beer and wine she wanted to finish off. That is all that I needed to hear. Plus, I knew she would have no problem with me crashing on her Futon if I overdid the wine.

At the time, this arrangement didn't strike me as odd. I had been over to Bridget's apartment on many occasions. But, now that I think about it, this may have been the first time that I was over without other people present. I considered us very good buds and, believe it or not, I was just looking forward to hanging out with one of my favorite people.

Bridget's apartment was great: small but homey, artsy yet traditional, and it had one of the most attractive tenants. She was the sweetest person I had the pleasure of knowing back in the day. Her living room consisted of a Futon, milk crates used as end tables, and an impressive entertainment center with surround sound.

Before turning on the movie, Bridget thought it would be nice to wind down by listening to some music while drinking on our first glasses of wine, all the while enjoying each other's company. She went in to her bedroom to change out of her work clothes. While she did this, I figured it may be a good idea to get my bag of accessories from my car. I always kept a bag of street clothes and all of the amenities, (toothbrush, toothpaste, brush, razor, etc.), in my car in case I heard of a good party to go to right after work. It also helped out whenever I picked someone up at the bar and stayed at their place. I just found it hideous to get back into my work clothes, from the night before, in the morning. It's always good to be prepared.

When Bridget came out of her room, the comfort clothing of choice was a t-shirt that touched the middle part of her thigh. "Wow," I thought to myself as she sat next to me on the Futon. "She looks really good in that t-shirt."

By now you are probably thinking: "This guy took advantage of this poor girl as she was getting nice and relaxed after a long day at work." I would be lying if I said that the thought didn't cross my mind on a few occasions in the next half hour. But I was not the one who got the ball rolling on this particular evening.

We started talking about music and some of our favorite bands. You know, we started getting into one of those long and drawn out conversations about everything you feel intelligent talking about when you begin feeling a buzz. So, we were getting into some deep talk when Bridget said that she needed to have her neck rubbed and asked if I would do it for her. She promised one in return.... Seemed innocent enough.

So I can keep this book at the "G" rating, I will skip most of the on going events. Let's just say that one thing led to another and we ended up sleeping together. The next morning, we spent a little time together and promised each other that our friendship would stay in tact. I wouldn't have it any other way. The friendship that we had built was very important to me and I didn't want to lose it due to us being careless this one evening. I felt good about this as I was leaving her apartment.

Remember earlier when I talked about the innocent flirting we used to enjoy while working together? Well, things were not the same after our erotic evening. One of us would try to get something going with it, and then the other would get somewhat offensive about it. This attitude also occurred when one of us would have an opportunity to go out with someone else. I can recall one evening when I had a girl meet me at work, so we could go out after I finished my shift. I ended up canceling the date due to Bridget getting weird about it. I would also not be myself when the tables turned and she was the one with the date. We had many conversations with each other to try to bring things to where they were before the incident. Both of us knew that we were better off as friends. But it was too late. After our might of ecstasy, we found it hard to be friendly with each other. I eventually quit where I was working and moved to a different bar. We saw each other a few times after this, but we could never get back to where we once were as buddies. We lost our friendship due to a shared curiosity.

Stop yourself from the agony and torture of a work relationship. There are good reasons why many corporations don't allow coworkers to date one another. You can't leave your personal issues at home when some of them are at work with you. Remember the motto: "Don't stick your pen in the company ink." It is important to stay focused and keep all your relations with co-workers professional.

3. PERSONAL BUSINESS AT WORK

Have you ever been standing in line for a while at the bank, only to have the teller close the window when you were the next in line? After standing in line for a good twenty-five minutes, that would tend to frustrate anyone. Then they come back five minutes later and tell you they had to take this important personal call, to finalize confirmation for a flight and hotel stay in Mexico. They told you how they couldn't wait for that week off, so they can tan and drink Pina Coladas on the beach in Cancun. Guess what? I could care less about their vacation to a tropical paradise. I have just waited THIRTY MINUTES, with five of those minutes waiting for you to re-open your window, so you could tell me that you were on a personal call about some stupid vacation? When and where did people, that work in the people industry, lose sight on what they were at work to do?

It's understandable that everyone needs to take some time off to relax and enjoy the paycheck that we work so hard to earn each and every week. However, bear in mind your responsibilities when you are earning that money—taking care of the customer. People who you do business with don't give a damn you are anxiously counting down the minutes for a vacation at the beach. People will ask when and if they feel like talking about the happenings in your life. The customers delegate the subject matter of the conversation you engage in. You are a puppet waiting to see which string will be pulled before making the next move. Considering the money your customers spend at your establishment, that's a fair deal. Letting them play as the maestro will reflect in the amount of tip they leave at the end of the night.

Perhaps you feel that you don't want to hear their stories because yours are much more interesting. "Who wants to listen to these sad sacks," could be your philosophy. Bartending requires you listen to these stories as part of your job duties. You are the sound board people need to have every once in a while.

Some people drink for some sort of reason, good or bad. The bar provides a place where someone is willing to listen to them, without analyzing the hidden meanings of what they say. They are also coming in to see someone that is always happy to see them and to be there when they are feeling out of sorts. Alcohol enables people to loosen up after a long day and lets them lose their inhibitions on occasion. This is another factor to look at when dealing with the public. Due to their state of mind, people tend to open up to you and speak their mind. You must show interest in what they have to say. You are showing no gratitude to your patrons if you are busy dealing with something not pertaining to work. Push your personal life to the curb when you are working. You will not have enough time for it if you are to do your job properly.

As a bartender, you are there to be the listener. You are not there to tell everyone how your day is going. Forget about you for a while. If you want to talk about how you feel, wait until you're off work and go see your own bartender. One point to remember is: You cannot make money listening to yourself talk. This is another personal issue that needs to remain locked up while you are working.

A major distraction, that you will see nowadays, is the use of personal cell phones at work. Working behind the bar requires you to do too many things at once to have time to talk to someone on your phone. These should be off and in your car when you are on the clock. There is no reason for you to have these on the loudest ring while you work. It takes away from the ambience that you are trying to create with the customer. That connection on your phone keeps you from being connected to all of the things going on at the bar. Too many steps already need to be taken to ensure good service. These things seem to slow the process down to a snails crawl.

One night after work, I had some time to go have a drink before going home. As I sat, patiently waiting for a drink on this particular evening, the bartender continued to talk on their cell phone while pretending to wipe down the liquor stock. After nearly an eternity, this individual finally realized I had sat down. She lifted her finger up, gesturing that she would be with me in a minute. Once this occurred, I headed for the door in a somewhat fuming state of mind. I had just used up all of my free time waiting for this individual to get done with something not pertaining to any of her customers. The bartender actually chose to finish her conversation before serving me! How dare they do that to a customer! No wonder the bar had a total of ten people in it. If the rest of the bar help was even half as bad, the crown had ran away and went somewhere they would be able to get a drink in a reasonable amount of time. As I was headed out, the bartender stopped me and asked what the problem was. "That", I told her, "is the problem—not having any clue why I was leaving."

I may seem a little harsh at times, but I expect the best of service from employees when going into any type of establishment. When dealing with the public, the customer always comes first. Nothing else matters. Serving the customers' needs makes them want to do business with your company. Think of yourself as a public relations person for the company you work for. YOU will determine if this patron will ever walk through those doors again. This should always be your mind set.

Boyfriends and girlfriends are doing you no favors visiting you hours on end at the bar. You are there to be the host of the party and be in conversation with all who enter the establishment. With the other halves there, you tend to want to make them feel comfortable and not be yourself. You will tighten up to where some of that outgoing personality isn't able to shine. Explain to them that you are there to be at work and you would appreciate only a brief appearance. Customers of the opposite sex feel uncomfortable joking with you when they are around. There's nothing wrong with innocent flirting with the clientele. How will you be able to do that when you will be spending half of your shift explaining to your lover that it is only in jest? Make them stay away as much as possible when you're working.

Personal matters should be dealt with on personal time. To effectively get work done, one should go to their job with an open mind and a fresh start. Do not lug your personal baggage with you into the work place. This only leads to problems. Personal affairs while on duty will stop you from doing your very best. It will also keep your job very insecure.

4. STEALING FROM THE OWNER

Something needs to be set straight before moving further into this subject matter. This "something" has a lot to do with this part of the book, so it's a good place to start. This is for all of the owners out there who work ungodly hours due to not trusting the employees that are employed at their establishments. I feel that bartenders, as a whole, have gotten a bad rap due to the few bad apples in the industry. If you are an owner, and have experienced some of these bad seeds, this is an understandable way of thinking. However, there are ways to go about finding the right type of employees to run your establishment. It will take you time to trust after getting burnt once. But if you follow some of the things that we are about to go over, you won't be digging yourself an early grave from overworking.

Talking to some bar owners, they feel the only way to ensure that no one will steal is to be in the establishment from open to close. This is not a healthy way of running a business. You might want to throw in the towel right now if your trust has waned to that point. If you do have someone that is stealing from you, you have to first take the correct steps to find out who that person is. Once you are sure that you have found the culprit(s) do the right thing by prosecuting these individuals. There are three reasons that this is the necessary step to take. First, it makes the other employees aware that you will not tolerate anyone stealing from you. If they had been thinking about it, they will decide not to. Secondly, it keeps the other bad seeds from infiltrating the bar. The last, and most important reason to prosecute is that you will have made your point with the workers, and you will have good employees from here on out. This means that you won't have to be there every waking hour. You can take time off to do the things you should be doing—like, enjoying the money your establishment will be making for you. This is why you opened the business up in the first place, wasn't it? Most have their own businesses to get away from the everyday grind of a 9–5 job. They are not getting into it by having to work 15–20 hours a day, seven days a week. At least, that would be my assumption.

You should have employees working for you that always have your best interests in mind. This will keep you from having to work more hours than are humanly possible. In order to achieve this type of staff, start by showing the same respect that you expect from them. Respect is a two way street. The staff will be more than willing to keep you informed of all things when you are not able to be there. They will also respect you enough to make sure that everything is being done by the book. The business motto "A happy employee is a more productive employee" rings true in this business. Give your bartenders praise every once in a while, but not so much their egos inflate. Just every once in a while say, "You're doing a really great job" or "The customers really seem to appreciate you." Employees want to know that the boss is noticing their hard work and likes having them as part of the team. This respect will crush any thoughts most people will have in terms of stealing, or at least should.

Of course, you will have those people who have learned to cheat the system. They will take advantage of anything and anyone to reach the goals that they want to accomplish. If that means taking a few dollars from the till, or not ringing something in so they can pocket the cash, they will find a way to take what's not theirs. How little do people with this frame of mind realize how much more fun and enjoyable work would be, if they were to do things the way they should be done—with honesty and integrity. As much as I hate to say it, you will always have that one person who will cross the line and do what they can to get away with this. So, it is viable to make this shady type the example when they are caught in the act—prosecute them.

For the most part, the bad apples will eventually get caught and fired. There will be many of the innocent who will feel the brunt of missing supplies until this individual gets caught. That is probably the worst part of it; even more than the loss of money for the establishment. Somebody on the team is making the whole team look bad. That is why it is important to let the owner know when there is something amiss. It will save a lot of torment down the road.

I am about to tell you a story that, believe it or not, is the exception to the above. The guy I'm about to talk about walked away with a load of the business' money and got away with it. From my understanding, he is still taking from the till whenever he gets the chance.

The greatest bar I ever worked at had someone that seemed to be taking money and merchandise on a nightly basis. I was the acting one in charge when this was taking place. Every one of the employees came up to tell me that they had, on several occasions, seen this person in the safe when he wasn't supposed to be. A couple of good people that we had, that told the owners, were let go soon after. This stopped anyone else from attempting to do the same. It was more than the workers that were seeing this happen. On numerous occasions, I had customers telling me that this individual would try to pass an old tab to them when they were ready to pay out. This only meant that he was going to pocket the money that was given to him by the customer; money which was supposed to be going into the drawer. If he got caught by the patron, he would apologize and say that it was a mistake; then he would ring up the correct bill. As many times as he got caught doing this, (quite a few), one has to wonder how many times he wasn't.

How can the owners not see this happening? If they did see it, why was this person allowed to be doing this, while having good people fired when the owners were told of the thievery?

One reason the owners seemed to be blinded was that they were only in the bar on a part-time basis. They would typically come in and open in the morning, and would be out by early afternoon. You see, I was only the acting one in charge due to the responsibility that I put on myself to make this place prosper. I was never given the title of bar manager. The owners did not want anyone having the power to hire and fire anyone. They also didn't want to pay the money that would be asked of someone with that title. However, I was there at night and was the senior bartender. I had to make sure things were running smoothly for my own sanity.

Despite their pronounced absence, the establishment did great business, due in large part to the commitment of the majority of their employees. The main core of the staff began working for this bar and restaurant when they had no business. We put many hours and sweat to build up the business of the bar because we felt we had the right niche and location to prosper. It took many broken hearts, including mine, to realize that the owners—who, at the beginning were so desperate to have something work for them—were turning their backs on the people who were the reason for the success of the establishment. This place had made it due to this commitment. Yet, they were firing these same people to protect this con man.

Now, allow me to explain the main reason for the blindness on the thievery. The individual who was freely taking from the till was, and still is, dating the owners' daughter. The owners blamed everyone else for the cash shortages and inventory except the guilty party. I guess they felt that blood is thicker than water. It pained me when I opted out of this place, because I exercised everything in this book to make it work. But, for the sake of my mental health, it was the right decision at the time. I guess it only got worse after my departure. They actually gave this person the title of bar manager!

This guy has since accepted a job on the east coast. Since his absence, the bar inventory is now jiving with the money. But knowing the owners of this establishment, they assume that getting rid of the people they did is what made the difference. Personally, I think they got rid of some very good people all because this low life is considered family. It's ridiculous how some choose to remain ignorant of truths they don't want to believe.

If the owners I am talking about ever approach me and inquire if I am talking about their establishment, I will say "Of course not." This would only further prove the validity of my accusations. I do hope that they one day realize what is happening and take the measures necessary to prevent it from happening again.

Stealing something that is not yours is not good under any circumstances. If you go against the code of ethics in this occupation, you deserve the worst consequences that can be thrown at you. Sure, stealing will give you more money than if you played it straight. But, your career in this occupation will be short lived. Keep in mind that when you steal, you make everyone else that you work with seem guilty until you're caught. I have been accused of stealing on a few occasions. What upset me most about this is that I was working beside someone who had the audacity to steal from the owner—and even more audacity to sit there and let others get blamed.

If you are getting into this business to steal, I have got a bit of advice for you: Don't you dare!! Our occupation is relentlessly ridiculed because of people like you. We are viewed as untrustworthy people with no ambition and are no longer considered a respectable sort. Bartending has some downsides due to what we offer the public, and we definitely don't need any more bad press. Working in a bar is a profitable occupation for those who want to put the work and effort to bring the right people for the establishment; this includes the right clientele and best employees. If you see anyone that appears to be taking what is not theirs, let it be known by the right people. You are not a rat; you are someone that does not want to get falsely accused of a crime you did not commit. Also, you are someone that wants to keep their occupation clean.

5. COMPLAINING IN FRONT OF YOUR CUSTOMERS

Psychologically speaking, it sure feels good to get things off your chest; especially when something wrong happens to you. A sense of urgency comes over you to discuss this incident with the person nearest you. This trait affects each and every one of us. People tend to dwell on what the negative things are, and feel a huge weight coming off their shoulders when they are able to share these bad occurrences with another person. As much of a human trait that it is, this should never be a bartender's practice. You should be the solid foundation of the establishment. Nothing can noticeably faze you, no matter how bleak things may seem. At least, that should be the view point of the people sitting on the bar stools. You are there to be their shoulder to cry on; to be the guy or gal who has it all together.

Of course, bartenders are not super human or numb from experiencing the everyday obstacles everyone else experiences. But, a good bartender will keep their emotions at bay while serving his people. Keeping their chin up while waiting on customers fends off patrons from asking "what is wrong". This question can lead to problems. Even if you can save face and insist that nothing is the matter, the person who did the initial questioning will keep asking you until you spill the beans. A whole slew of complaints tend to unravel as you release these inner demons until they are all out. This will only make you feel good temporarily. Then you will realize what you have just done. You have thrown a rock into the middle of the pond, only to experience the disturbing ripple affect it will cause throughout the bar.

Once you start nagging, it's hard to stop and before you know it you will be diving into a rampage. Who wants to come in and pay to see the guy that's serving them bicker about the bad things that happened to them on this particular day? Complaining just keeps bringing you down even further, so you can complain even more. What's the fun in that?

I'm sure that at some time in your day, someone will approach you and inquire how your day is going. We all do it every day in our lives, many, many times. This is something we do as second nature. Usually the response is short and sweet. You both exchange pleasantries and go your merry way. However, on occasion someone may be more willing to divulge their disastrous day with you and all its glowing details. Shortly into their tirade, you feel the sudden urge to run as far away from the conversation as possible. Asking someone about their day is a common greeting practice facilitated by nearly every person. But in most cases, you really can care less how they're doing. At least, you don't care enough to here a five minute story about everything going on in their life on that particular day. That's exactly how a customer feels at your bar. Customers come in to ease the everyday chaos in *their* lives—not to hear you talk about how bad your problems are.

When asked how your day is going by one of the patrons think of something pleasant or fun to talk about. Forget about the annoying, irritating dilemmas fresh in your mind waiting to explode at any moment. Practice the mentality that the glass is "half full". Someone, at this very moment, is having a far worse day than you can ever imagine having. Realize that many people would give anything to be in your shoes. It is much too easy to focus on the negative aspects of our lives and what things irk us. As a bartender, you should always provide a brighter spot for your customers—something they can look forward to in their otherwise drab lives. Talk about things that are not so personal or important in your life. Choose lighter conversation to entertain the masses.

Burnout, something that we have mentioned on numerous occasions, is the main culprit of complaining. Tenders seem to lose control of their emotions when too many hours are spent serving the drinking public. You need to know your own limits when it comes to hours spent behind the bar. This will ensure you will keep your best face on when you are in front of the customers.

One common thing that people in this business complain about is the way the last bartender left the bar. Either they didn't cut enough fruit, forgot to stock the bar, etc. You, yourself, would be surprised to hear some of the things you forget to do when you work behind the bar. This is one thing this business never lacks—the constant complaining about something or someone.

Griping in front of the customers is not recommended at any time. It doesn't matter how close you get to some of the regulars coming in. It is not their job to comfort you when you are feeling a little grumpy about something. It is never good to complain about the other workers. This only makes them look bad to the people coming into the bar. It also takes away the good feeling that people have about the establishment. Complaint topics can also include the time it takes for food to come out of the kitchen, the quality of food in general, or just a lousy life altogether. You are making the place you work seem like a place they should not be coming to. You will probably lose some good customers by giving them the idea that the establishment is not up to par.

If you have a problem with a co-worker you should tell them so in private, so you don't embarrass them in front of others. No one likes a moaner. If you don't have something nice and warm to say then keep your trap shut. Remember that negativity tends to linger. You will have a hard time ridding the bad taste when you start the nagging.

Keep in very clear that we, as bartenders, are there to serve the public. We welcome the people into our business with open arms and a positive attitude. We must keep the smile on our face and have a positive outlook on life. Keep the memorable experiences in the establishment only positive for the customer. Bad ones will keep them from coming back; good ones will keep you on their list of things to do. So, keep your chin up and smile.

SUMMARY IN A NUT SHELL

By now you can see that it will take more than knowing what type of liquor goes into a particular drink. If you follow the rules and try some of the things that I have discussed in the previous pages, you will be very successful in this business. As in anything in life, you will need to work at being what you want to become.

The topics that we have discussed are seventy-five percent of this occupation. Anyone can learn how to make a drink. A true superstar in this profession will know how to act and react in certain situations. Just like anything else, you will need to experience it first hand before knowing what you are getting yourself into. You must have self-control and much discipline to truly be given the title of bartender. You will be tested, throughout your career, on how mentally strong you really are. You will fail these tests on occasion. After all, you are only human. But, the true showing of strength will be how you handle these miscues and learn from them. The errors you will have will only make you stronger and better rounded.

Let's go over some of the things we have already talked about that will give you the success that you will be striving for:

1. **Learn the basic skills of being a bartender**—This is a team oriented occupation. Do yourself a favor and be the shadow of the most experienced and most popular person of the place you work. There is a reason why they are so successful—Learn from them.

2. **Be a professional**—Act the part when you are behind the bar. You are there to do a job.

3. **You are in control**—Make the room your own. When you work there is no doubt, in anyone's mind, who is in control.

4. **Everyone is your buddy**—Be a friend to those who take the time to come in and see you. They will come in to be part of the festivities with your other friends, (clientele).

5. **Be a good listener**—Everyone needs that lending ear to release some inner thoughts. You are there to be their sounding board.

6. **Pour a good drink**—You will benefit those you serve and those you work for by keeping the drinks to the recipe. This will benefit you by keeping the inventory on base with the sales of liquor.

7. **Know your customer's drinks**—This will save you time by knowing what people drink when they sit down at the bar.

8. **Promote your establishment**—You should be the biggest seller of the establishment. You are there to grow the crowd. Do what you can to attract them in.

9. **Know your competition**—It is always wise to know the goings on in the other area bars to learn what works and what doesn't.

10. **Be an entertainer**—You want to keep them coming in after you have lured them in. People want to have a personality behind the bar. You are there to be their entertainment.

11. **Be ethical and responsible**—You must know what you can and can't do to follow the laws in your state. It's important to follow the rules. Not doing so can cost you more than your job.

As we have learned there are some things that you must stay away from when you are working at a place that serves liquor. Listen to yourself before doing something that could jeopardize the rest of your career.

Here are some of the things we discussed that you must avoid when working in this business, or any other for that matter:

1. **Drinking while you work**—Control the craving you may have to tip the bottle while on the clock. You will lose control of your place in a hurry if you try to keep up with the clientele on a nightly basis. If you feel the need, give yourself a limit. This will keep your motor skills and decision making where they need to be.

2. **Relations with your co-workers**—You will change the atmosphere of the place you work once you start dating a co-worker. You must stay away from this to keep everything at work professional and stress free. Personal affairs should never be associated to the work place.

3. **Personal business at work**—You are only taking away valuable time from your customers when you do things at work that have nothing to do with what you do there. Keep all personal affairs away from your place of employment. You are there to serve your customers. This is your number one priority.

4. **Stealing from the owner**—This is the deadliest of sins of any bartender. For all of those who feel that this is just, I have no use for your type in this business. Those caught in the act should get their day in court. Prosecute the ones who do this. This will keep others from following suit.

5. **Complaining in front of the customers**—The clientele should see everyone working at an establishment as one big, happy family. Customers don't want to hear the griping. Go somewhere in private if you need to discuss something negative to a co-worker. Public areas should be one big bed of roses in the eye of the patrons.

You now have all of the fundamentals needed to become one of the elite in this very exciting occupation. How rewarding it will become will be up to you. I have only given you the strong foundation to build from. It will be up to you to make this occupation what you want it to become. You must want to grow from the insights that I have just shared with you.

No matter if you only are doing this as a part time thing, you should want to make it as lucrative as possible. Just dealing with the everyday happenings at the bar will make you become stronger at whatever you decide to make your career—many years after setting foot on the other side. You will be better at dealing with the curveballs life will throw at you on occasion; all because you learned the most valuable part of this occupation—the human part.

Part IV
THE PERSONALITIES

A unique thing about bartending is that it is one of only a few occupations which enables you to have conversations with various types of people within the same room. There will be those times when you will find yourself encountering the type of people that you want to avoid like the plaque. However, in my years of experience, these types are few in comparison with the good-natured souls that you will have the pleasure of knowing in your travels. People tend to display their true selves once they see past your job as the server of their drinks—rather as someone they can trust and confide in. Having a few drops of spirits always seems to eradicate any inhibitions someone may feel. After knocking a few back, the bartender has become the customer's friend and confidant.

This chapter on personalities is important to place as a chapter of this book. It will give you a window to peek into prior to being thrown to the wolves. Without going above and beyond as a bartender, and to know the inner workings of the public that will come into the establishment, how can you expect to impress the majority of the customers that come in to see you?

As a bartender, your character must be adaptable to the many personalities that will frequent your place of business. Think of yourself as a chameleon. You must be able to mold yourself into a situation and the person that you will be conversing with at that very moment. Any lack of understanding or positive communication with a customer could potentially drive business away. After spending some time behind the bar, you will come to know the personalities that I speak of. Until you gain that much needed experience, this chapter will come in handy to prepare you for the many different traits that you will be exposed to.

We all have our own distinct personalities. It's something that makes each and every one of us unique. But despite these differences, there are ways to break it down into groups of characteristics shared within specific people. For example: from those who are very social and control the group, to the wall flowers that want to remain in the background, only wanting to be part of the group.

If you enjoy the art of people watching as much as I do, you will have some fun trying to place your customers into these various groups. Most of these traits delve into some of the fun natured and not so fun natured people that you deal with in your everyday lives already. This chapter will provide you with a clearer picture of what you will encounter when you get on the other side. This also demonstrates that you are not alone when you find yourself dealing with some of these types of people. I can almost guarantee that you fit into some of these yourself. I know I do.

The following types of personalities which will be discussed have derived from my personal experiences working as a bartender. These varying personalities are easily identifiable to anyone who has spent time in a bar, whether as a customer or an employee. To keep this an easy read, I am only going to discuss a few of these characters. You will surely be adding to this list. These personalities are what kept this job interesting and kept me hopping. Without these characters, I would have probably not lasted long in this career. It definitely made me realize that I wasn't the only odd character out there.

Keep in mind that, to be great in this line of work, you have to have a keen understanding on what makes different personalities tick. This will be of benefit for you to reach the ultimate goal: to be a great bartender.

1. I AM HOLIER THAN THOU

In the minds of these individuals, we are strictly there to serve them. If they have a ring to kiss, then by God you should kiss it. I list this group in front of the others for a special reason. You treat this type of personality much more differently than you would treat the general public. They are the exception to the rule—just serve them. They do not want to have any conversation with the bartender. You are beneath them. Just make sure you don't forget anything that they ask for. They are looking for anything to complain about the service you have given them. This may sound harsh. But if you have had any experience working with the public, you will agree with my insight about this personality. Do not expect more than a standard tip with these folks, as long as there were absolutely no flaws in the delivery of their food, drink, and demands.

This characteristic can come from any of the rich, middle class, or poor patrons that come into your establishment. Their social status means nothing, so don't think I'm only speaking of the monetarily fortunate. Some people, who go into places that service the public, feel that they should get their money's worth and treat the people serving them as their own personal servants. They forget that this individual, serving them food and a drink, has the whole room to keep in mind when they are doing their job. They believe that they deserve undivided attention at all times since they are in the bar spending their hard earned money. Everything you do will be micro scoped. Every little error will cost you a percentage point or two on your gratuity. This is from the "generous" fifteen percent that they feel is only for perfect service; not the twenty to twenty-five percent you should be receiving for having to run around with your head cut off, trying to meet their every demand.

No matter where you find yourself employed, you will have this type of personality. They will be the first type you will be able to define, because they stick out like a sore thumb. They will also be the ones who will make or break your day. You must keep an even keel and keep strong when serving these types. Otherwise, you are only feeding their need to feel that they are better than you. Do not put yourself in that position. You only tend to look out of control if you let them get to you.

Every Sunday a couple from the neighborhood would come to the bar I worked at for Brunch. It became a weekly routine for me to come to work and see their car parked right outside the locked front doors. The couple would sit by the doors to wait for the bar to open. I would get a little frustrated every time they would show up early because they would complain about having to wait outside while I set up the bar. I remember thinking to myself, "You know we open at 11am! Stop coming here ten—thirty minutes early if this bothers you." They didn't seem to care that this bothered me; it was our fault that they decided to show up early. It always started my Sunday off on the right foot.

Once the doors would open at eleven, we would be able to serve food, but were unable to serve liquor until twelve. In Ohio, the law stipulates that you cannot serve any alcohol until noon on Sundays. However, these particular patrons would complain at the notion that I had to wait an hour to serve them their Bloody Maries. They felt it justified that, since they were there every week, that we should bend the rules to meet their request for drinks with breakfast. Just so I wouldn't have to hear them gripe, I would give them their coffee on the house until the witching hour, so they would have something to wash their Eggs Benedict down.

As for the Eggs Benedict, they were never right! Too bland.... too much salt.... too cold ... I think you get it. Never did a week go by when they were completely satisfied with all aspects of service, food and drink.

For the longest time, I thought the owner of the establishment put these people up to this to test my patience. However, one particular day, he had the pleasure of sitting next to this couple at the bar. After hearing the abuse that I received from them and only receiving a ten percent tip, he looked at me in astonishment and proceeded to congratulate me on my demeanor. "They would have been out on their asses on day one if I was back there serving them." That's all I needed to hear.

The following Sunday, the wife of this couple seemed to be having a bad day. She decided to put all of her happy and considerate personality out on me. She didn't let up on one thing; every single thing I did was wrong. As she was complaining about her food for a solid minute, I looked behind me as if I was searching for something on the floor. To get my attention, she yelled, "What are you looking for?!" That's when I leaned over the bar to get eye to eye to her and stated, "I was just looking to see if your dog was behind me. Because I know you wouldn't be talking to me like that." That was one set of customers I was happy to never see again.

In this occupation, you are there to be a servant to the patrons that fill in the seats in your establishment. You are getting paid to take care of their every whim and to keep everyone satisfied. However, you are not there to take care of only one group of people. This needs to be understood by the several groups that you will have in the establishment at one time. There must be a bending and a mutual respect that comes from both sides of the bar. If you feel you are not getting that much needed bend from the customer, you do not need this type of person or persons as a customer of your bar. You will tend to lose sight of the big picture when you try to adhere to all of the demands being beaconed by this personality. When this happens, you forget about the others who depend on your service, as well. You WILL lose this type of customer eventually. You will never completely satisfy them, and they will go elsewhere. It will be their loss. They will hopefully come to realize that there is no such place as that perfect place. When serving them, just be sure to keep every other patron at the establishment satisfied.

2. THE SOCIALITE

This type of personality can usually be spotted in the center of a large crowd. They want to know and be part of every other individual at the bar. You will even see them occasionally walking around the dining area to sit and converse with the people enjoying a good dinner. This type of personality would fit perfectly as a bartender. But, these great folks have decided to act as an ambassador to your establishment instead. It's nice to have this type of person as part of your place. However, it must be stressed that you need to stay away from befriending this person too much. This is where the characteristics between this type and a bartender are much different. As a server to all those who enter your place of business, you should never share any stories or secrets about the other clientele with this individual. They have a tendency to share these with other customers. Keeping secrets to themselves is for naught. People occupying the barstools will no longer hold you as someone they can trust with personal information. As a bartender, you do not want to be looked at as a gossip. Might as well look for another bartending job in another bar.... in another city!

Not that these individuals are doing this to make enemies. It is quite the contrary. They just want to be part of everything. In there minds, there is nothing less than all involvement in the establishment. They want to know that they have the acceptance of every person that they come across. To do this, they feel they need to share things with others that should probably not be shared. This type of personality feeds off the fact that they are getting attention. To get the attention, they will try to get approval from the information they possess, good or bad. They don't consider the ramifications until it's too late.

I had the honor of having a patron that would follow me from the various bars which I was employed. He would usually come in at the beginning of my shift and would work the room—introducing himself with people he was meeting the first time. He would then proceed to make them part of the group. This kind of exposure for any bar is the kind you couldn't pay enough for. Yet, there was one of my long time followers, spreading the word for me at the bar. He was the best public relations person for the establishment—at least for the first six months of my employment at an establishment. He had that type of personality that everyone seemed attracted to. He was very easy to get along with and always had a good, funny story to tell. People had a tendency of sticking around for that extra drink when it was known that he would be coming in. He just seemed to have that charm at the beginning. However, he would seem to need more than just that after a while.

It would seem to happen about the seventh month every time when he would begin to wear out his welcome with the regular clientele. He had a tendency to get too involved with other people's problems and would find himself right in the middle of the chaos. He would then proceed to share these problems to anyone that would listen. Not a good thing to do, especially when stories get blown way out of proportion at the bar. He didn't seem to understand when it was a good time to share stories with others and when it was not. I could sense when the end was near when customers would begin to complain about their new friend. I would also see the people that would stay for that extra drink would maybe have one less if they new he was coming in. His once funny stories would start to get nothing but eyes rolling in disgust. I think he would sense this happening once it got to a certain point. After getting himself in too much hot water on various occasions, he would disappear until I would start working somewhere else. By the time this would happen, this was a sigh of relief on my part. Not that I didn't enjoy his presence, he would tend to get too close for some people. That would make me a little uneasy. It was nice I didn't have to say anything to him when it was time for him to say goodbye. He always seemed to know when it was time to make his exit on his own.

It is easiest if you remember this about this personality: They not only want to be your friend—they want to be everybody's friend. To do this, they feel the need to step over the line on occasion, to get the approval they are looking for. You just need to be aware of these types to keep yourself out of trouble with the other patrons.

Other than the reasons stated above, these folks will be a great benefit to your establishment due to their outgoing personality. It's like having your own PR person at the bar. He does all of the introductions for you. He is a host to your establishment. The groups that he introduces to each other will tend to come in together and will continue to grow, long after this individual has done their magic. There will be a sense of camaraderie that will be present due to the outgoing personality of this individual. Keep this type of personality happy, and you will have a loyal customer for life. You will also have a busier establishment.

3. THE JEKYLL AND HYDE SYNDROME

We touched a little on this in the "Ten Things to Be a Great Bartender" section. This type of behavior happens to those people who have a few drinks too many and lose control of who they really are. You get to see one person walk into the bar and a completely different person walk out after having a couple of martinis. There are two extremes you will see when this happens to these types of people. Some will relax and loosen up with a few drinks, while others tend to tighten and flare up after knocking back a couple. Drinking tends to be somewhat of a "truth serum" to those who fit this personality. Their inner most demons seem to become exposed when drinking certain spirits. Demons may not be a good term when defining this characteristic. Some people tend to get a little too frisky and loving when indulging with some of their beverages of choice. Why do you think there are so many wedding chapels in Las Vegas, sin city? It may not be a coincidence that the amount of liquor consumed in this fine town seems to top the charts in any region of the USA. I find myself wondering how many sober couples actually tie the knot in these places. I guess a book could probably be written on this topic itself.

There are also the types who, when sober seem reserved and to themselves most of the time, blossom into the wallflower of the room. They become the life of the party that everyone can't seem to get enough of. Regarding my friend that I mentioned in the "Be a Professional" rule, she would have fit that description perfectly. However, she happened to change her mindset in front of the wrong people at the worst possible time. In her case, she lost her professional demeanor while on the clock and lost the respect of her boss as well as her clientele—At least those who were not involved in the body shot segment of the night.

Some individuals who fit this character tend to become the biggest bullies when consuming too much alcohol. These types tend to have a chip on their shoulder and dare you to knock it off. Something in their lives has given them this sense of hatred that they leave in the back of their minds until they have the excuse of booze to expose it on occasion. Though you will find some people wanting to cause havoc the moment they step into an establishment, most of these types are not expecting to become the asses that they will become when enjoying a few spirits. But, once the liquor is added to the equation they start to turn into something that you cannot accept in a social environment. They begin to act upon the inner thoughts that they can usually hide when not indulging in spirits. And before you know it, you have a full knockdown brawl on your hand due to someone saying something that wasn't politically correct at the time.

Knowing 911 comes in handy in these situations. Do not try to take matters into your own hands! They expect you will come in and be the Calvary. This only fuels the fire that has started within your room. Once they get to a certain point, there is no off switch. You must get the police involved and get them officially thrown out of the bar indefinitely.

Here's a great example why you don't want to be the hero or say something that will bring out the worst in people. It occurred while I was working at a place in Dallas, Texas. This bar was a very happening place on the weekends due to the live entertainment that we were able to bring in. On the weekday nights however, it was rather slow on most occasions. I happened to be the Tuesday night bartender. A few college kids from the local university would come in to visit me weekly, and play some pool on our one and only pool table. On this particular Tuesday night, it happened to be so slow; I was able to join in on a few games while socializing with my only patrons. The only other employee working on this night was this Mexican gentleman who I will call Manny. Manny spoke very little English. That didn't take away from his skills as a fry cook. I experienced some of my most memorable meals at this place. He made the best burgers I have ever experienced, to name only one of the many meals that seemed to taste best at the hands of this cuisine expert. I will never forget his smile: his two front teeth were capped in gold. I would say that he was probably in his fifties. He worked very hard in this place so he could send money down to Mexico for his family, as well as keep a home in the States.

As the customers and I took a brief break from the pool table to take a drink and share in some conversation, a couple of brawny guys came in. After getting their first beer, they headed for the pool table to play a game of pool. One of the college kids told the new customers that they were in the middle of a game and they could take on the winning pair. The guys who just entered would hear nothing of it, saying that the pool table was now theirs. You could tell that they were beginning to feel the beers from the other bars that they had visited.

Trying to be the humanitarian, and to keep the only regulars that I had on Tuesday, I jumped in and said that they could put their quarters up for the next game. They would have to wait their turn for the table. That was a huge mistake.

Let me give you a good picture to put in your head to make more sense of this story. I am tall—about six and a half feet tall, but when I was younger I was very lanky. These two guys were as tall as me and twice my build. They could have passed as a couple of linebackers. I had a tendency, when younger, to not know when to keep my mouth shut. I would not allow anyone to walk all over me. I could handle my own within reason. However, I got myself in a few situations that could have been the end for me. This would be one of them.

As I was trying to explain the rules of the house to one of the goons, the other put me in a wrestling hold while the other grabbed my legs. Within a few feet from where we were was an empty fifty-five gallon trash can that reeked of old beer and some vomit. How can I be so descript with the aroma protruding from this receptacle? Within seconds of these guys taking me down, I found myself head first inside this thing.

Once they had me cramped in there, they began hitting the side of the trash can with the house cue sticks. After what seemed to be a good two to three minutes of torture, the hitting abruptly stopped. In complete silence, I thought to myself, "These guys are going to pull me out of here and finish me off outside." That's when someone slowly pulled me out of the trashcan. As I lay on the ground, half dazed and in a fetal position, I looked up and saw my cooking friend, Manny, standing over me with that million dollar smile. In his hand, he had an iron clad skillet. Taking more of the room in at that moment, I noticed these two lugs lying next to me on the floor completely knocked out. Manny had just saved me from having to go to the hospital this night.

After the police took these two bad guys away, I thanked my friend by toasting him with a couple of beers. Not really understanding too much of each other, I thanked him the best way I knew how by buying him a couple of cervezas. I was very fortunate someone had my back in this particular instance. I don't know if he realizes how much I appreciate what he did for me.

There will be times when you will have to stop fights so your place doesn't get torn up. However, make sure to call 911 as soon as you start seeing things getting out of control. It will save you from getting yourself hurt or quite possibly killed.

Most people have a lot on their plates and try to stay focused on the tasks at hand when going through the motions of the day. This is my reasoning for the sudden changes of personality with these types. Drinking tends to drop your defenses on hiding your true feelings with your everyday life. Of course, depending where you are and how you feel about life will factor in on what type of personality will come out when you drop these defenses. I would say that a majority of your crowd will change somewhat when drinking an alcoholic beverage. It is your job to make sure that the change will be a good one.

4. THE CASANOVA

Every bar will have a customer who has slept with their share of the other people that will come into your establishment. The ultimate goal for these individuals is to see how many people they can shag. This characteristic loves the chase and the excitement of it is what keeps them going. If someone will give them the time of day, they will do anything possible to close the deal. This is where the term "One Night Stand" derives from. The chase provides a sense of gratification for these folks. Once they have gotten their prize, they will be on to the next victim. So, if this isn't what you had in mind when they have made you their next target—watch out!

The bartender is this person's number one ally in terms of keeping past victims and present other halves away when they are about to pounce on their next victim. To them, you are the lookout to make sure the close is clear so they can begin their serenade with the next naïve person who they find to be interesting. You need to be very careful not to fall into this trap. It can get you in a lot of trouble.

You will serve only one function for these "Casanova" types—you will become their excuse guy or gal. Be sure to make them aware up front, when asked by them, that you will not lie to someone asking for them on the phone, by telling them that they are not there while they are on their next mission. You will find yourself in the middle of something that WILL be very bad. The married Casanovas will get caught eventually. You do not want to be part of this. Do not make this your business. So when the other half calls, hand them the phone and let them make their own excuses. This next story will help you understand why.

I was working at a downtown bar that brought in many professionals for happy hour. One of the regulars I had was a defense attorney that appeared to be sleeping with all of his female clientele. Every time he came in, he would have a different girl with him to drink with. With each drink and every minute that would go by, this silver-tongued lawyer would seem to ensnare their interest to the point where the women would seem to be willing to take their clothes off right there. I have to admit, I was a little star-struck by the way he could talk these attractive girls into sleeping with him. This guy was no prize when it came to physical attraction. I guess the money this guy portrayed having was good bait as well.

You have to picture this guy to get the full laugh out of this story. This was your typical middle-aged guy, (on the older end of middle aged). He was the type of guy who drove a Ferrari as a status symbol. He was going through his second childhood, I figured. It became a joke to all of us working in the establishment. In fact, we would make wagers on how long it would take for him to coerce these women to go to the hotel with him.

One thing that my lawyer patron asked from me was to tell his wife that he was not there whenever she called. Being young and naïve at the time, I felt that it wouldn't hurt anyone by telling this little fib on the phone. Plus, it would probably hurt her to know what her husband was doing anyway. So, I became pretty good as his excuse guy.

On this particular day, things began the way they normally did. The attorney brought in a new girl and he began his voyage to the promise land by feeding this younger lady her favorite cocktails. I received the call from his wife about an hour after his arrival. She asked if he was there and I gave her my usual response of no. He was getting close to getting where he wanted with his companion anyway, so he didn't really have time to talk.

After calling me everything in the book, as well as some words that I have never heard, she then informed me that she was right across the street at the pay phone. If he did not come out of there within the next minute, she was coming in to pull him out of the bar physically. Since he was at the point where I couldn't get his attention, I poured myself a drink and waited for the fireworks to happen.

When she entered the bar, I would have taken her as his daughter if I didn't know otherwise. She was a beautiful lady who most men would do anything to get within arms length of. First thing I thought when I first saw her was that he was one lucky S.O.B. How could he ever want to cheat on that? The poor thing was probably one of his victims that wouldn't go away.

Once I got back to reality, I noticed that this woman was ready to take on everyone at the bar if she had to. She gave me a look that had me searching for a dark corner to cower in. As dainty as she was, this did not stop her from making everyone step aside as she headed toward her destination.

As she came up to the newly acquainted couple, she introduced herself to her husband's female friend and gave her a ten second head start to get out of the bar. Seeing the look that the rest of us did, she did not hesitate. What happens next is what still gives me chills to this day.

As he was beginning to conjure up a good story, she picked up an empty beer bottle from atop the bar and proceeded to beat the living hell out of him with it. Slowly, since I felt this punishment seemed just, I walked around the bar to stop this from going any further. Once I got to the other side, she caught me coming towards her and warned me to get back where I belonged or I would be next. With my tail between my legs, I finished up on the dirty glasses I had at the sink.

She then proceeded to take his family jewels in her hands and began to squeeze. She ordered him to begin walking towards the door, all the while not giving up on her grip. To this day, I have yet to hear another grown man squeal like that.

Well, that was the last time I ever saw this guy. It could have been embarrassment, or maybe he decided to straighten his way of life. Quite possibly, he went to Disney World to do some voice overs for your favorite characters since he found a new octave. She may have even killed him. To this day, I don't know. From that day on, I no longer lie to spouses or other halves on the phone. Next time, the person on the other end of the call may not be as easy on me.

Do not put yourself in a position to be a scapegoat for anyone, no matter how much you like them as a customer. Don't look down on these types, however. A bar IS a social place. Some of the people that come in are looking for someone to fill a void in their lives. It is not your place to stop this from happening. Just don't be the one to tell untruths to the person's significant other. You are there to mind your own business as much as possible. If anything else, just shrug your shoulders if asked any intimate questions. You really don't want to know.

5. THE STORYTELLER

It has always been fun for me to go into bars and hear other patrons discuss their worldly wisdom. You would be able to write a book the size of an epic if you could remember all of the stories coming from the bar the last month. Alcohol tends to bring the storyteller out of most of us. Without these stories, there would be an empty space in your establishment.

A majority of the public feels the need to enhance the truths of their lives, to make their stories that they tell more entertaining. Storytelling is a form of entertainment. That's why we have movies, television, books, and so on. We wouldn't have these things if the mass of people didn't find other people's stories so interesting. Most of the clientele like to hang out at the bar to get the newest gossip or are there to pass along some juicy tidbits of their own. It's always fun to hear about other people's lives. It makes you realize, as crazy as your life seems, you are as normal as the next guy.

One thing that you will come to learn, if you decide to come into this occupation, is that most of what you hear is BS. Most frequenters in your establishment have a B.S. in BS. Not all of the stories you hear will be fiction. I have described some stories throughout this book that are absolutely true—(okay, I may have tweaked some of them a bit to make them a little more interesting to the reader). But, we will sometimes add a little spice to our everyday lives by throwing in a few fictional events when telling someone a story that we want to share. Otherwise, they might not seem to be as eventful to the person you are sharing the story with.

Another form of storytelling is delivering the right timing on a joke. It takes a lot of skill to tell a halfway decent joke so that you have everyone at the bar spitting out their last sip as you are getting to the punch line. Anyone can tell a joke. It takes someone who works on delivering it with perfect timing to make it always sound funny and fresh. This is a skill that should always be honed and constantly worked on.

Being quick on a comeback is another type of entertainment at the bar. No one did it better than a certain waiter I had the distinct honor of working with. We were working together at happy hour one Monday night at a downtown bar. A group of councilmen would regular the place on this day after their weekly meeting. They would get a few pitchers of beer and discuss some of the topics that they went over at the meeting. On this particular evening, there was a fowl odor coming from the draft beer. I heard it mentioned on a couple of occasions prior to the arrival of these regulars. By the time that they had shown up, I completely forgot about it.

The above mentioned waiter happened to be one of the main attractions for these guys coming in. The politicians and he would quip at each other all night. It was fun to watch both sides give each other a hard time. This was all done in jest, of course. This waiter was a roly-poly type guy who you couldn't help but like. When he worked, we were always busy in the dining room.

When the civil servants received the first round of beers, one of them yelled at the waiter to come back over to the table. The customer voiced, "Hey, this beer smells like shit! What's going on here?" That's when my co-worker exclaimed, "Oh, sorry about that … I just let one go." Of course, I happened to be taking a drink out of my coffee cup when I overheard this comeback. The coffee went down the wrong pipe, and I choked for a good five minutes, all the while the customers were rolling around in amusement. But, that gets me to thinking. Were they laughing at his comeback, or were they amused about the guy behind the bar spitting coffee through his nose?

No matter what type of personality you have at the bar—be it the storyteller, joke teller, or comeback artist, keep this in mind: They are saving you, the bartender, from being good at all of these things by having their presence at the bar. It will give you the time to make sure that all of the patrons, who are enjoying this type of personality, are always filled with their favorite beverage and are given the service that they will learn to expect from you—as their bartender.

6. THE CON ARTIST

There is always a character in any business that needs to be looked at closer than the others and this one is it. Be it the sleight of hand, or sleight of mind, this type of individual has only one thing in mind. They are looking to deceive their victims.

Con artists come in many shapes and sizes. They can look like the poorest of the poor and the richest of the rich. They will seem to be something that they are not, so they are very hard to spot in the beginning. It will take you a couple of times being taken by these characters to know what to look for. There is some good news to this. You will become a little more street savvy the next time you are confronting them.

One thing that I have learned is that when someone is trying too hard to make you like them, the more likely they are trying to deceive you. So, that is one trait you can look for. Not that everyone like that is guilty of anything. It just will make you look at this person a little more closely when doing any dealings with them.

I had one guy who would come into the bar every so often. He seemed to be a very nice guy and would strike up conversations with everyone around him. Little did I know that he was checking the place out for his crimes. Knowing that I was the only one working at the bar on certain nights, he would wait for me to go back to the cooler to grab some beer, and then he would pull tips out of my jar without anyone looking. I don't know how many times he did this before he was caught. However, I was a little more careful with my tip jar after that incident. This same guy was caught down the road a few months later. We actually got him jailed for six months after the second incident.

Don't feel sorry for these people. They make a living taking something that is not theirs in the first place. When I worked downtown, there was a group of beggars that would take shifts to ask people for money when walking by their corner. It was finally learned that these three beggars had a very nice house in the suburbs. When the police went to check it out more closely, they found over $100,000 in cash stuffed in a wall. These people made others feel sorry for them and were living probably better than the people that were generous enough to give them something. This is when you need to ask yourself: "If I needed a dollar for food, would these people that want money from me give me a dollar if I was in need?" I would have to say the answer to that question would be a "NO!"

Sleight of hand is very common in the bar and restaurant business. That is because the con artist will wait until you are busy before attempting to take from you. The thing you must pay attention to is what type of money you are receiving from someone. They will give you a ten dollar bill, and then turn around and tell you that they had given you a twenty. The best way to stop this from happening is to keep the money that they give you out until you give back change. That way you can show the person, who tries this con, the bill that they had just given you. You must protect yourself by being aware that this can happen. It definitely will if you are to ignore it.

Now for the bad news: You will find yourself working with con artists on occasion. Look at the people that you see in the news. You will actually have people, who are in high positions within a corporation, taking things that are not theirs. They don't even need the money. They are doing it to see if they can get away with it. In the position that you are now in, and the responsibilities that come with being a bartender, you will find yourself looking at people a little closer. If you don't, you could be found as the guilty party for something that you did not do. ALWAYS cover your backside. You have to be aware of your surroundings at all times. If you are not, someone out there will take advantage of your weakness—trusting others with what you shouldn't.

There is another con game that is common in the bar world. This one is one that all of us have probably tried at least once. To the people doing it, it isn't really a con game. However, you can get the bartender in a lot of trouble if they are found guilty. Many young kids not old enough to drink will somehow acquire an ID from someone of legal age, or could possibly get one that has been altered. Being a bartender requires you to have the skill to know when an ID is real and when it isn't. You are not going to catch all of those under aged drinkers. It seems the more complex the real ones get, the more real the fake ones get. However, try your best to be aware. All it takes is for you to take a couple of the fake ones away from the kids. The word spreads like wildfire. The kids will lose hope and will find another bar to con.

Just a bit of advice when entering the bar world: Always keep your eyes wide open and be aware of your surroundings. Being in this business takes more than that first impression when you are dealing with people. Look at people as you would an opponent's hand when you are playing poker. They may be good bluffers, but eventually they will have to show their true hand.

SOME FINAL THOUGHTS

There are many things to learn when you step on the other side of the bar. Putting the "drink making" aside for a moment, I'm optimistic that I have given you a much more rounded view of this occupation. I hope I didn't scare some of you off when I mentioned some of the chores required for you to do, or the bad things that can happen to you. What you will finally come to realize after some time is spent in this profession is that there is much more fun and sun then there is bad and drab. There will be more than enough time for you to enjoy the other facets of this business. Where else can you be a host to a party four or five days a week? You will actually get paid to watch and talk about sports, meet new and interesting people, and have people listening to your two cents on occasion. I felt it was important to share some of the things that you will have to achieve other than knowing how to make a drink. So, I hope this opened your eyes a little more.

When entering this occupation, you are going to see a different type of world. You have to experience it first hand to appreciate this lifestyle. When you do get the opportunity, you will understand what I'm talking about. If you do this job correctly you can become the person people come in to see, and make more money than most people do working their career jobs. You will meet, and get to know, some great individuals you would otherwise never get the opportunity to know in any other type of environment. Not just one type of person; many types that will give you a better understanding of what makes this world so interesting.

One of the advantages of being a great bartender is that you can go anywhere in the world and find a job. If your passion is the sea, get a job on a cruise liner. If your indecisive on where you want to live in the world, become a bartender who moves to a different location every year until you find the place you can call your permanent home. If nothing else, it will give you the life experiences that most could only dream of having. What other job gives you the freedom of doing this?

The thing that made me stay in this profession so long is that I didn't want to feel that I was stuck in an office, Monday through Friday, in a nine to five job. I wanted to experience different people every day. This job gave me the opportunity to pick up and go to the next adventure, in a different part of the country, not knowing what to expect next.

There are many job openings in this occupation. Do not fear if you start your career in a place that doesn't suit you. It will be up to you to make it the type of bar, which you enjoy working at, by bringing in the clientele you will feel comfortable with. If that still leaves you uncomfortable in this particular place, move on to the next one. You will find that most bartenders will move around on several occasions to find the one that suits them best.

Do yourself a favor and talk to some people that have experience in the business before taking the leap. If they are successful in this environment, they will tell you the things you need to do to be the same. Do not fall in the trap of being just a person that serves drinks. Always make adjustments to make yourself better, so you can experience the most that you can in this profession. It will pay you back ten fold in the end.

978-0-595-46697-9
0-595-46697-4